T0121319

Geoff Feiling/No-D
CECI EST IMPORTANT SEMI:

C'mon Dark

iUniverse, Inc.
Bloomington

iUniverse books may be ordered through booksellers or by contacting:

iUniverse
1663 Liberty Drive
Bloomington, IN 47403
www.iuniverse.com
1-800-Authors (1-800-288-4677)

ISBN: 978-1-4502-9915-2 (sc)
ISBN: 978-1-4502-9916-9 (ebook)

Printed in the United States of America

iUniverse rev. date: 03/11/2011

INTRODUCTION: BRIEF SYNOPSIS OF "GF"

So, Geoff was supposedly born on June 11, 1981. Geoff was supposedly adopted; Geoff finds this fact of his life very pliable to his situation. But Geoff really does not think it matters, because no matter the crap Geoff spews on a few various occasions such as government funded holidays, he loves his adopted Mother, Father, and Aunt better than anyone else, he is just insane, which is also a very pliable, yet a very real excuse for many of Geoff's actions or words. So, Geoff is insane. Well, what is wrong with Geoff? No one figured this out, and since Geoff is now practically thirty years old, Geoff faithfully takes his medicine every night, for the peace of mind of those who care about him, although the pills do have a certain negative effect on his phallusist reactions when a sexual interaction presents itself to him, but he really does not care too much about that anymore. Geoff has been taking anti-depressants, anti-psychotics, and nerve pills since he was about 10, and he believes these psychiatric "medications," have dissolved his internal sex-drive to practically nulen-void. He also believes they have made him become a mental "health" junkie in the severest of terms, because he can tell very easily when he does not have them, and needs in his body to swallow, as long as he has his drugs, he really does not need sex in the physical way. Geoff is one of the very few people around, who regularly buys pornography magazines for the articles, and his sad ass is telling the truth if someone were to ask him, but he does enjoy the Halloween issue for the pictures, the beauty of women found in pictures utterly evil, beauty and chaos, Geoff digs them, but does not rise to the occasion.

*

Paper or plastic? Grocery work is Geoff's employment, and it is the perfect cover he needs for his operation. Geoff gets all the free lunchmeat his little belly can handle, and he does enjoy it, but Geoff does not need to "indulge" himself on the simply human concept of taste or nutrition for any longer. You see, Geoff knows it is his mission to keep his tact ness with his obviously foreign correspondence alert the most he can, yet needs to keep his front of acceptance by them (human majority) polished, though most of them (the human majority) view him as a person clinically insane. But he can get by and stay out of hospitals (mental), and there are even a few of them (human majority) he associates with, though most of them are part of the class human majority minority, or outcasts affected by things within the human alien mind. In Geoff's math that aspect of many is so much more detailed than the shitty system the Romans put into place, though many of them were forbearers of Geoff's power, he does not mention them. But Geoff may in fact, not be smart at all, since he has not found any total harnessing of his alien being.

*

Geoff did not have a natural birth; he was not conceived in the normal sense of people making love. *(Rape, incest, or bestiality, either).* He considered for a long time he was a product of one of these human aspects, also that maybe he was supposed to have been an abortion, or maybe was a giraffe until he turned 25 years old. But he was in New York City for a very brief time, and one early eve when sitting in a coffee shop alone, he got his orders from his real boss, who appeared as a female alligator the other customers did not notice, only in New York. It was from this sterile female alligator; Geoff learned many important things he needed to do to complete his job in the city of Pittsburgh PA, which is where he lives, but his place of residence will be determined by the pupil-less eye of the system from the outer limits of the useable galaxy he comes from, which he requested to me (the reporter for this piece) shall remain nameless, as well as myself.

POOL-BOY APPLICATION

House me and make me you. What I meant to say was house me and make me work for you, I will be you're houseboy, and I will be your pool cleaner, too. I know this sounds very nice to you. I have been living here in you're house for so long, and I love you and cleaning pools. What I meant to say was I love the smell of females, as well as of cleaning products. You are very beautiful. So was my mother, but differently. *Employ me*? I will mean some thing important to you as well. *Employ me*? You're breasts are perfect, filled with vindictive voluptuousness, I will dream tonite of giving medical massages to them. Oh, you must indeed think I am silly. I would really enjoy massaging you. *Employ me*? I have … *(ahem)*… credential powers in my box of green jelly-beans! ***Employ me***?

INVADE YOU, WE WILL. WE ARE PROUD OF OUR PROGRESS.
War: Extended Hell

Grab me in the neck, think about your country. Choke me to the death, make my eyes pop out so you can arrange them on your flag. Give me some time, give me some more time, it has only been nine years since we saw each other. Paste the eyes, bide your time, because the vengeance we continue to show from those 9 years ago, shows not rebuttal but an American selfish changeless consequence… as it has been for years…

\ SPLIT PERSONALITY EXPULSION /

You good to go, go. Don't come back, we're gonna set a trap, like a hunter. My personalities know each other and we do not like you and kick you're Irish ass on out, don't come back when you get work, because we already know you are going to join the government!

SENTIMENT OF REALITY

O LORD!!! BLESS ME WITH MYSELF.
FLY BY NIGHT – FROM THE FEATHERED TAIL IN MY HEAD
DEVIL CARES.AND CARES FOR YOU.LORD ME DEVIL MY –
UNITE IN PASSION AND ALWAYS SEE THROUGH.

RAVEL, MINGUS, OR <u>LOVE ACQUISITIONS</u>
As well as: My way if I was to have a kid.

Good, I am glad you sittin down. You have to be sitting for what I'm about to tell you.
I dig your presence, you jive as jazz. I have never met one who has feeling
which is so much similar to mine, could it be true?
You kind of remind me of my mother's love, kind of a sketch of HR Giger,

and I think it is pretty cool that we agree on what is positive in life, but I also enjoy our disagreements.

We both know we hear we both know we see, we both know we hurt, but for an end to the feelings naturalistic ness, we never hope their cease.

I keep a log of each thing which hurts me, pain is unpleasant, but has remained <u>our</u> most functional learning experience…

As well as the things we saw that any being of sane disillusionment would not ask to see. We know we can find strength and learn to deal with it from absolutely any other breath, present, far gone in mind philosophically narcissistic loving living divided conceited repulsive angry enticing laughing enjoying pleasure sizing, pleasure dividing, **PLEASURE DRIVEN,** humanistic, class systematic, classless and communistic. Reality driven, with eyes for our future.

We know these things, but we do not waste energy concentrating on them. They are what are.

We are proud; we do not go to great lengths to show it, though. We get high…

on life, we'll have been here when we're dead.

We'll have "tripped" on life somewhat, and we'll know it was a "good trip." We'll know this on our death beds, before we reach righteous fate of beautiful death, life anew, basked to the air of evanescent nothingness. No memory, no being. Like a mosquito on a naked thigh, crushed upon his blood withdrawal attempt upon his immediate injection. But it doesn't take a lot to leave a little, an orchestra of actuality, a bass in a smoke crowded room. Or leave a human actuality who knows who they are, blood is thicker than memory, if the blood is prepared, blood can be evaporated, but it'll fall right back. In a lifetime, in any time, there is flesh but no ceiling. And vampires shy away from our dirty blood, our blood does not evaporate… no energy, no life giving, vampire sustenance… but life making of another child who will grow and never have the fear of trusting themselves to Vampire Existence… but O, we are here, we repel the Vampire who are the majority, and our scent of the strongest as humans repels them aghast.

You see this pride too, you will be mine. We are stinking up the worlds that need a little
stink with the humanistic notion of taking notes on what is.

We cry, we cry for where we're at in our heads, the fact that we know that we aren't.

But we have proven them wrong so many times – we put ourselves above them.

Or – maybe we know it, and we know perception is mere reflection to them, which is as realistically shattering as the glass of the poorly made mirror they put together themselves with generic glue bought in blessed Prospect Park upon the stone's strike. All 3 of us know well, common mental health would be beneficial if the idea of changing self-perception was made less eminent

People need to learn to take things as they come, and deal with themselves through them, and not the junkie business of mentality meds, once you're on, you can't get off, and these drugs screw one out of so much, it hurts worse to try to kick, kids. – *Son, don't cry or get angry, or we'll dope you and hook you, every night you will have to hit...* and DO NOT try to kick, kids. Problems will be made worse, but the kids will be worse on themselves when Dr ***** starts the hook-up, but they won't let the boys and girls at school know it, he'll lie – kids are honestly perceptive, but the drugs make the "patient" lie to them because he cares about their image of him? No... because he does not want to get hooked by the doctor on another horse-pill. Things may have changed since this experience of mine, maybe, maybe not.

Me and you, we're maybe gonna have a kid... we take sex for what it is, what happens... happens.
We know we will not be perfect parents, but if the baby screams, we will not put his head in the sink, we'll make it into a tape, mix it in with Ravel or Mingus.
We'll tell her what she can't do, but not limit her by telling her what she can.
We'll teach her, always. She'll go to public school, you and I know it will get her ready for the world's unfairness, but we will be fair to her, because we both believe everyone should learn there are a lot of good people on life's beginning ending nothing trip. Music will always be on in our residence, mainly Ravel, Lou *(Reed)*, Mozart, and Mingus.
But we will not consciously conceive a child. But life happens – it is what it is.
We will teach her pride, the
magic of words – the bea-
uty of music...

We will accept the challenge of giving her the reality
of never trying to be anyone besides her/
him self. And one must
B

honest – first and foremost to one's self.

Okay – Love, this be our plan, we do it, we shimmy we confuse. None of the PTA
or censorship Moms or Dads like us… another majority we will
                              valiantly never be a part of. But we'll
learn notto get too proud of ourselves for
                    B-ing together.

.
Life happens. So does shit, but life isn't shit, life is what one makes it.
You have to spread the stench, log it, blog it, and bring it to
places which it should be, but isn't. Life's
                    love turns the pungent wreak of it
 into an aromatic fragrance(!)
        Ravel orchestras and the Jazz Bass of Charlie Mingus.

Heh, that was funny.
I think what you said was something like – *September 11, 2001* was totally unexpected. It was also good when you stated that you never thought for something so serious we, as a country would never make the so simple, yet so effective mistake of invading a country and killing kids from the country that had not an honest grain of any effect on us being attacked, but seemingly so few compared to when after the president declared that the battle was won, to how many thousands of our young and older military people who were sent to "win" and told they "won," the president made this statement on a yacht, and it's funny you were surprised this is when the honest war began, it's funny common sense did not make you at least contemplate it happening. It's humorous as well that when you elected a democrat to the office, and he started another war as well as continued so many, and many more died and are dying, you had the false guise that your party would make something different happen, maybe stop the killing, and you are only now learning that American politicians are the same all around. But I am glad you voted – it could have been worse, but it's still bad.
I think it is funny you are sixty years old, and these facts are only showing themselves to you, now. Soon you will realize – you will never be able to do anything about anything that happens in the country you love, and *"good people"* like us will never have any kind of control to make change, stop wars, change the world, but keep the fact that at least eventually you realized this, and died being <u>yourself</u> instead of a member of a political party – like O, so many. Die with <u>reality instead of affiliation</u>. Peace will come to you, if you accept the world will never be a peaceful place while

6

we're here. Acceptance is the way to peace, it is harder, yet the most honest order, and you will feel like you achieved a positive state by learning this. War is part of the human condition. This is a detestable aspect of it.

It will take some time, and frustration, but it's funny, because humor is the grain of sugar you have to imply this perception with.

And maybe you will be able to see how funny you used to be, using the false condition of loving you're country so much that you trusted it, now you love you're country still, but you feel a lot better loving the right things about it, and having the common sense of never trusting any politician…

You are still funny, but you are honest and realistic.

People should not die for **ANY** reason forced and illegitimate.

IN THE AFTERNOON:

The night is dead, what soul is bad? The red sun and blue mist of morning will come to this life again. The morning died, the day remains longer, but dies long before the night. *No soul.* **Flesh** and **mind**. Disgusts in the day. Blood in the light. The day is alive, but pain ceases, die in the wretched day, become alive with the beauty of the stars and moon and blackness, and the sight awkwardness of the beautiful death of/in the night – time of the vampire – time of life in death in the earth time entity end of the day. *No soul.* Fumigation in belief of spirit or self. Lifetime reality will try to rid each one of this notion. Blood red moon, deviless genuinity, godless philosophy. *No soul* in the day. Reality's presence is only acceptance and not hard to come to in the least. Common sense prevalence. *Spirit in the night.*

The night is dead, the day is dead. No *self* is bad, soul destroys.

The day bleeds, the night feeds on blood.

Finding the positive power in this thought teaches us the power in reality, our progress of perception.

This day is impermanent, yet it will rise again.

Beauty in darkness gives one this confidence.

THE BLOB
Written in a No-D mind
I. INTRODUCTION

Dreaming and dreaming, so decide on an extravagant mission to write a litany…

Hah hah… Hell hit me, sky on the up-swing, Pittsburgh night. Remember that time graciousness flung it's blackened liver substance
blobs on my head?

Well, me neither, no matter, this time at this moment I will describe it to you piece by bloody piece – the depths of her veins, pulsing blue flowing with blackness.

The day prior the blob (Introductory "epiphany)"

Pah me Patty, love my city-style and taste the earth of my drawers, Lola.
This was what I was thinking in the morn, in the morn –
the morning
Of twilight red blood sun cancerous beauty,
the weaker side of the moon.
But seemingly in the minute, still minutia but mysteriously substantial light.
(Sound of Faint laughter in – in the air of my distance)

II. THE APPEARANCE

Right back… my mission was to come back to my pad, something sheer was annoying me on the outside, *in my head, in my head,* on the outside, sometimes anger shows off her brazier more to me while outside,
but it was like half horse, half squealing rat, something indeed internal.
The outside at times is worse than inner alone. I am
often slightly annoyed when I do this – self strain can occasionally
bring about negative emotion, in one of thee's negative actions.
(hurt)? (human)?
(I have always found high
pitch laughter –

Some-
What…
An
n   o
ying)   maybe Anno
yin-yang.
Up the road down the road – up the road up the road. Heh heh heh, quite a trip –
Happiness with my self, love, if you will… feeling good, put
on some Miles Davis. Listening, licking my lips, what's that?
There is something black and giggly on me tennis-shoe. Hm.
Try to kick it off. Giggles like a liver after 2 boiler makers and eggs.
So it moves with itself – but is not moving from my shoe.
I wonder to myself, to myself, if it is a mutant snail.
Living in these times, I noticed snails resemble

pieces of livers, and it looks like a human liver piece
on my shoe. A black one. Just to make sure, my liver is
still in me, I check, and my liver sends a cooling
sensation through my body, just to let me know he is still in
there.
Always been a good liver,
tells me when he goes away for boiler makers and eggs.
Anyway, I'm thinking it's a snail,
so I let him hang out as a personal fashion statement, as well as my body as
tree, to myself. What the hell?
                    (This is a blob, I do not realize this, yet)

III. ATTACK!!! ATTACK???
I sit on my reading chair, symphonies playing. Look at my Andy Warhol
prints on the wall for a bit, say to myself, "hey man, myself, man, Marilyn
Monroe sure was a New York Devil, man, Warhol proved it."

        The blob does not move. Look down to the cracks in the chair,
little blobs jumping out and landing on my lap. Weird, really weird. Blobs
on the floor, man. Blobs everywhere, honey/I know they are not snails.
Wow, am I tripping… I have not smoked any weed
        Since the quaint above middle of September, hey it's cool. I know
these
are blobs, in my mind on the floor, on my walls, on my lap, my mind is
rough, gets funny ideas – so –
I decide these blobs represent the female originality which to me seems
threatening. And I decide I want to attack them back – but they are stronger
than I.

Loving them is my guerilla attack.
*(Blobs Blobs love the Blobs, capitalize the BLOB, Blobs will never die, and
no one loved them so, I begun, and the snails are still woman, and have
grown teeth and pinch my flesh,*
And they all have mainly pain and discomfort to give me,
*And strength and respect, thestrength of beautiful elegance learned and
leaned , most*
*effectively displayed because it is the mark most elegant in the woman
species*
of those who have lived and died and die every night…

Well, like anyway, what I'm saying is women, like, are so much more tough

than men, and they
apply it so mondo- firm, unretro, like blobs is me, like your little admirer
stealing a kiss I, totally never
had, and my blobs bite, my women who look at me one time and say –
"Love me, but thou' shalt be-est my enemy, divine another one for me"

"(dry gum in your teeth with all of its strawberry flavor remaining... blow
one more bubble, skank)".

GRAVITY HAIKU

Gravity pull me back. Gravity, natural, but I know, I know, I put it there myself. Gravity pulls me back, but it is my mission to rise above it, and keep my thoughts. Gravity is challenge. These four sentences were not haiku, but my version of a Buddhist sentiment.

ANOTHER...?

Don't like it. Wouldn't care if it never came back.
But like you. And it'd be great to see you again.
Never understood you or it.
Don't know if I want to try. I doubt it…
but still don't know for sure. I'll get around, either
way, call it faith, I don't like that word, though.
I guess one could say I have this in myself.
I am trying to deal with me, as me, the best I can…
but I still have a hard time dealing with loneliness at times.
What is wrong with me? I hate you,
but I need you. Your eyes are an ocean of perfect and fixtured mist.
But each time I try to start to speak with you, I either
embarrass myself enough to get out of the situation,
or I say something that I shouldn't without realizing it…
but I know you are the only human who understands me.
Grappling the issue of me with another is a hard trip to take.

DREAM WITH ME

Dream, do not dream of me. This is an order.
Dream of Penn Avenue, the Allegheny River,
or the memory of the Bowery (Bleecker Street).. Dream of her or him,
or Auntie. Dream of permanence in the world's
population. Dream a little dream, dream it for me.

Dream the past will be there eventually.
Dream the dream of worldly peace.

Cancel the wake of the day, turn the light
into the dream of life, dream of time unwasted.
Cancel a dreamer, cancel the scheme of desire. Dream a little dream, live
inside mind for me.

Dream your time is now, here, dream.
Dream something different. Dream what is, instead
of what could be. Mind's eye from sounding time.
Use your senses, take them with you to sleep, and you might find,
you are a lot like me.
Dream a little dream. Do this with me.

HORNY

I am filled with silent terror as I look at your breast. Oh, your breast, so
pretty and peaceful under your tank top, a white one, and your breast!
Smooth, mature, one I would love to clench in my right palm, and to suckle
each freckle, each vein, and lick them, oh I would lick them. I would kiss
your permanent frowning thin lips and run my fingers through your mat
of animalistically perfect red hair, I want to lick inside your ear, taste your
pink lobes, by nibbling, I shall nibble your pink lobes. Oh, your breast!
I would let my hand sway over it until both of your mature nipples have
goose bumps, and I would suckle the blood red privacy of a time well-
forgotten. Oh *beauty*! Oh, *savor*! O, salt upon my lips from the sweat on
your breast! Timeless in equity!!! I hate my life… I hate my thoughts/no
I don't, but I wish to suckle enticingly your enticingly erotic breast! I will
say anything to get you to accept me.

JUDGELESS JUDGE

Don't get me wrong, I wasn't saying anything insulting, well; I wasn't
saying anything I thought should be taken by you as insulting, to you or
me. I really, don't try to insult anyone as whole-heartedly to the point where
they know they are being insulted, I even rip on myself abstractedly so I do
not understand it… I probably would cause myself to have some kind of
breakdown if my self criticism was direct. Other people as a majority, well,
maybe those excluding my mother, view me as clinically insane anyway,
so they never really put much thought into anything I say. So I know I am
not hiding my insults from them about them with a sense of "intellectual
superiority," they just know I am off my nut anyway and just rambling
again.
But it really was not an insult when after you said you couldn't meet me
on Carson Street next week, then I said I wished you could, and the look I
gave you, might have looked semi-sarcastic, an "I don't care gaze", maybe

angry, I don't practice my looks for situations like these, or any situation in the mirror. I actually use the mirror as little as I can, so I don't know how it looked… it had to look a semi perturbed or disturbed though, because not a minute after, you either lied or didn't to me telling me you and your boyfriend were taking your kids to some amusement park.

You were probably telling the truth, but I wasn't surprised you either told the truth or lied.

I would really like to hang with someone like you, someone who would be as easy to talk to as you, maybe you, someday…

But what you said did not really bother me that much, about not being able to go down South Side with me on my birthday…

This kind of thing has happened so many times in the past, lie/truth whatever, but how women seem to need to stop the conversation, my heart hardly sinks at all anymore. It's like a rubber-coating has formed around it.

Sometimes, like with someone I want like I do you; it's a foam rubber coating –

Takes a minute to bounce back, but does, slowly…

In exactly one week I will be one year away from 30 years old, and have never had a someone who didn't use me like a siphon. I guess I'm "*jaded*" however inexperienced I remain… it would be nice to have someone to start the year with… my head will try to form words to try again, but I am not one to doubt my past experiences proves that it is more than likely a goal will not be achieved…

I don't trust myself, but I would love to trust someone…

And I would never insult you, I am too lonely…

I just do not understand.

FANTASY INTERVIEW

Cool down man what's your style?
I can't cool down, I can't cool down.
Hey man, what's your style?
Say what? Man, what's my style? My style is to study, my style is to drink espresso, my style is to purposely poison my own well of writing, then try to get the poison out, not all of it – there is a need in the writing for at least a few drops of contamination, don't ask why, I'll answer nonetheless – I am indeed blood poisoned, lucklessly poisoned, and therefore I feel the need to write. It is better therapy than even the sessions I conduct with a split personality I have learned called Sigmund Freud… but I try my best not to write about only a singular poison that dwells in my crimson entity blood of myself – in fact – I am going to affix the question I just asked

myself – with the ever so perceptive question of …and what are some of these poisons I write of – but I'm gonna state it real metaphorical like – or I will state them *really* identity like – I'm telling you a lot, doc – but at the time I am trying to make you think – if you can discern these poisons, Dr. Pad of Insane Scribble – I plan to stop having my one on one session with my other personality, Sigmund (I call him Ziggy, he calls me Dr. Feiling), any way you take it, here it goes – my poisons…

Everything I write has poison in it, sometimes too much and I have to edit a large piece out, but I write what I feel, I write with honesty, what I have always tried to do with somewhat of the strength of my father I hope I inherited, though when he tastes some of my poison, he does not even try to swallow. I really can't say I have been through a lot, though I have been through some negative aspects in this life trip mainly put on me by me, I write about them, as well as the main negative aspect IN life, but how I know it CAN be positive. I used to Powel drive myself with the bad, and was sent away, away, too many times – so I learned I had to not kill me often in the physical sense anymore and it took some time to kick the habit of wanting to die like a snake decapitation, then it took me even longer to quit wanting to cut and burn myself – I still have the marks of my selfish masochism – but I quit doing it, first mainly because I did not want to freak out girls, when one seemed a possibility which proved nil anyway. But then I started jotting my poison onto the page and I realized through myself and he alone – it is really a lot of fun… and I loved it and wanted to get better at it so took to reading everything I could pick up, even if I could not understand it – I started Rimbaud when 13, so really, anything that I seemed to identify with whether or not I could get – am I rambling? So I didn't do the mutilation thing any longer.

Then – supposedly on May 11, 1997 when supposedly I was fifteen, (that age interacts with the year) – but according to the hospital reports or government or whatever my brains were lying in the street and I had surgery – I was jacked by a fantasy lady with glasses, I met her, and steal money from her monthly to this day, though she served her complete time in my mental prison, where she wrote books on the subject of her glasses and minivan. She was saving money for a while in my "bars," only meant for my mentality towards the situation. The brain loss caused severe depression, and I was lost, friendless and still slightly am, though it is improving, but depression still weighs on me often, depressive manic ness if you will, but it helps to write about it.

Then there's the women, luck, luck for this Irish fuck never shows it's retarded head at the right times. Never had luck with one of the higher species, but would love to and still try. So when I see a woman or talk to one, obviously – you know me, jellybean, it always ends negatively, though

I wish sometime I would 'hook up' as us modernists call it… and I wish it a lot… and I try… but I get left in their peripheral sight every time.
So maybe I have not seen a lot, maybe I just have bad luck – Luck, No Luck, No Touch – so this shits with me and I write about it, masturbation is too loss-conscious, really.

Write, write, it's not that good, but it may make sense to someone, but life's not always acceptable to me, so I do what I gotta do. I write in spasms of what some would call psychotic gibberish – but I really don't think many people from my present view me as psychotic. But the past still rears it's angel wings of insanity every once in a while and someone will bring up my wasted youth on me… but no part of either one of my parents was in the least a wasted part, they love me and continue to teach me, as I write this over and over again. Honesty may not always be the best policy when writing, but it is important to my writing and everything I say are my honest feelings, and it is important to include my parents, but in the end, it turns into poison because I realize they are the two people who can put up with my bullshit, and even respect me for some of it… and I do love them, and my cousins who are the only people I ever wished I had as brothers and sisters – family is basically all I have known and I **AM** lucky in that sense, doesn't help my loneliness for something more – so in the end that turns the <u>cheese</u> of my life into the mold in my write.

And I don't like the USA government, and so many, not all, but so many cops – both because of the seemingly permanent or lasting betrayal of the last and greatest human dream of sensible needed enforcement as something as possible yet unrealized and unrealistic because of us humans – and an only titled as the enforcement of peace, making the pop stand of this town or this country a peaceable controlled business, it may not even be a dream anymore, but acceptance of a control nightmare, that you have to do what you have to, to just stay out of control's way.

Nothing to say? You're no good, I'm outta here, but those were my issues, now you know.

FAITH IN SELF
Devils here, we got plenty devils here.
Devils black, with nails like shears.
Devils are sharp; devils ask and learn their place in life.
Devils are honest, and sometimes they even smile.

No horns, no forked tails nor colored violent red.

14

No evil inherent, but the knowledge life is what it is.

No concealed hatred, or anger, but no recompense for those who hurt them.

But no meaning less grudges, we know these emotions reconcile with the body's

early death recaptured, and emotion stated only in decay, can kill a man.

Bide the time of a life, and dig what you can from it.

I gave a first person response to the ceasing of the grudge, but that ain't me.

I have a lot of grudges, and I know I'm not the only devil here and know for damn sure I ain't no angel…

But I do acquire an education from my grudges and gripes, and much from my good feelings…

And any education is never wasted, and I am proud to take no biblical or non form…

Sometimes it is hard, but all in all – I know what I have to do to live sanely,

And I will die at least semi-naturally, and I'll get by – it's good to have myself as a belief.

Life's what you make it, or break it into you're fitting, and it ain't a bad trip.

I promise to this entity to live of every moment.

And I'll see you around, I hope I do.

QUESTIONS

Ever get to your birthday and you did not think you were gonna make it through the past year of your life at midnight on the eve?

Did you ever think your life was filled with lies of extravagant beauty, to make you believe when the diseases of life hit and you was about to split, you lived well, so you could give yourself some kind of notion of pride in yourself, since the diseases of mortality's hearth which, in reality are mortal life itself?

Did you ever doubt your birth certificate, or think it was only implied, and you were born a long time before?

Ever hope someday to believe anybody's good intentions?

Ever thank yourself, but at the same time curse yourself for your paranoia?

ACCEPTANCE: BRIEFLY

Mind the facts, learn the memory, bide your time, destroy you're enemy.

Learn the facts, history does not repeat, memory is useless, and as disposable as old meat.

Mind the history with this in foremost thought… crank it up, rock and roll, make history, use it for you, dissect good intentions, keep one eye to the side.

Try, what one can do instead of what one has to for survival here, don't bide time but take it, live to ability, be dead when you die.

Do not destroy you're enemy, make them live with themselves…

Life happens once, die when you're dead.

(timeless entry)

TATTERED SCATTERED THOUGHTS ON ALIGNED SUBJECTS

1. Past Lives:

Think about the transient reciprocal self the dead inside self of now dead again, delivered, endeavored chimney clogged arteries of the space you tried to call your own on the divisive intrusive night in the South Carolina wetlands and the stupid, stupid things you did there.

SITAR/JAZZ BASS/MANIC FLUTE/80s GUITAR RIFF

2. Idiot person in the modern mental health system in America:

Turbulence powpow**POWA!** = too little appreciation – I love your life – but the thoughts you have expressed to me – are genuine – and I am one who believes in fulfilling your deepest desires – just don't blame me. I tried getting to your middle to help you through your dilemma of self – but I also can handle me a lot better than you can you – you do not want to believe other folks got shit too – and you know the world revolves on an uneven rotation around you and the frogs in your socks will not stop biting – you know all of this, and you have shown me no sign of improvement –You are a terminal fool, and you are a headache and an annoyance, I will not offer the slightest remorse for saying this upon your death. Next time I'll be seeing doc Flutson Polinkwo, I'll be getting the darn toots out of here – I had it, you didn't – only the strong survive, I will be transferring from this little place…

To a career in bag-packing therapy…

This was my advice to you, you asked for it; maybe it was like a test…

Or maybe I am trying to get you to leave me alone…

But I'm not saying I WANT you to end your life

Maybe I'm saying you should think about requesting the tabloids, playing some cards, just quit complaining like a thirteen year old boy who legally can not run for president, but for some reason, would really like to, it amounts to the same thing – in pointlessness – complaining and viewing dreams that are impossibility are alike in this respect. Dreams can be funny, they work sometimes. Complaining is like trying to build a castle out of an orange rind… and I listened to entirely too much of your watercolors trying to lather the glass dripping into puddles from your life brush of personal impossibility, and your plain stupidity upon the slightest application of a "good" intention…

And I'm getting out, so get out of my face now, go annoy a therapy man or something – god knows more than half of them deserve it a lot more than me –

And if you ever do trip on out of here, we'll both change the locks on the doors and mess with the system as much as we can – but this is not happening – so I don't really care. Nor for you or what you decide to do – I am not saying I want you to die, I'm not saying I care – just stay out of my face – I'm on my way to my space – and your weakness is disgusting…

And that is all I'm going to say about that.

Jazz drums/ Fugazi blast /Shakuhachi

SCREAM

1.

I have watched strong minds, plagued by indifference, pull of life, divisioned indifference, discrimination uponed, with the thwarted grace of an angel…

annihilating themselves with nothing other than acceptance of their weakness.

The main people who put me through the hell I have been damned to, O, I accept and find honesty and joy, in the penance Hell of realism life tried to kill me with,

so distant, but filled with the

grounded sense of self one must possess to achieve life brought through the
            challenge of an unheard voice, hours of directed/misdirected hate, drunken years destructioned division between the separate entities in one –
            Insanity, acceptance, life/death/self.

Who become affected by the dream of pain before things actually happen to them, years of hospitalizations filled with free candy and basketball between therapies, kids who don't
            know much, but at their early age, hear the menacing
                  voice of their implication
            in the world placed upon them by drugs they are   prescribed – the manic beginning
                  of finding a shapeless entity that they are told to try   and try to put a shape to, and
to find shape in what is most beautiful often in what is not there,
                  because to them it is a notion of being someone other than themselves.

Which in reality is the common point that defies the more, maybe not natural, but indeed realistic and charming need of the must to accept the beauty of chaos…
in themselves and the world of reality…
      Hidden because madness in
      my time was treated in a way which tried to prove its lie.
      Unacceptable ness pointed at the patient with a goal to   have him/her view this of them self…
            Ignoring the point acceptance of who you are and   where one arrives in reality is best met with finding sense in it, and who are drugged and divided further by the system of mental health, and spend the rest of their lives in institutions for things that the system made them feel such as chronic anger, or suicidal and dangerous thoughts… who are told to forget the dream of former human feeling, that the world is not corrupt… and to forget their past instead of try to learn from it.
(Thursday, June 10, 2010) (2:50 pm)

2.
Granted, you were the first ones the ones who wanted me physically, or claimed to.

Who took me into you're room, with a similar name as I, we played rummy until an hour before lights out, then you said you wanted me, to fuck me, and you were absolute in your idea we shan't be found out – a little pumpin' behind the juvenile bars, where the last thing the shrinks would suspect is a gay inquiry, you're skinny bone ass driving spasmodically into my overweight even more crazy self, but I said no, I was not "into that" at the time, though you did awaken a curiosity that would be fulfilled by me... though one I could not maintain it as my goal, but still feel at times, would make a "love life" so much easier.

Who screamed like a wench the day before, and was not seen until the next night – a slightly big blonde curly hair girl – this night we played cool around the "doctors" and managed to get enough leeway – and you brought me into your room, I was a "model patient." And we talked of our madnesses, yours seemed practically dangerous, but I was diggin it. suddenly you crouched on the floor, and asked me to make you good... your pants you rolled down, your ass was nice, and you looked upon me with eyes of the mad I knew so well from looking in the mirror and seeing my personal "depth of death." But I said no, I was tryin to think with reason and your deep abortion scars... well I didn't like that... plus you probably had some kind of disease, which I did not need.
I still ask myself the question whether my nature or common sense in these 2 situations
were a point for me, or another goal against me scored by the other me.

Who bought into the idea of death/no life for the mad – the "professionals" still try to sell me.

Who was in a mental joint with me, indulged me slightly with a love for Stevie Nicks, talked to me like no one had...
So about a month after we cut outta the clinic, I run into you on the bus, on the bus, in downtown Pittsburgh, while I'm coming back from The Point with brother briefly Engine, so I say hey, wassup, you doin anything... you wanna come back to my place for a beer? You agree, us 3 get to Brentwood, almost in my ghetto, and you hit on me... and like the inexperienced dolt I was, I was like, wow, this never happened outside of a mental institution to me, I seemed to take no mind of the fact that in one of these places was where I met you... so I'm like hey, you wanna kinda start going out? Actually you said that, pussy me only agreed. Idiot me agreed. Didn't realize sometimes madness can be dishonest, just like the system

that has hurt me so much, and that you were a sly bitch, using me like a quarter grain for a fiend, and you mutilated yourself and she who deserved life more and put the hurt in my kitchen sink… but I learned, I learned, not to always take to the cut of something as unique as something which never occurred before, and what's cool is though my hands grip of you screwed with me – I was not surprised – the scab of reality on my eyes did not lift. But it did bleed.

3.

Unity is not permanent, times and minds change and fade like watercolors on glass.
Life of humanity is not permanent, but semblance is a combined human aspect…

Semblance is something human, the realest form of godliness.Connection is not permanent, correction never is.
But Connection makes the road less jagged, and can make some things seem good,

Or even permanent.

Like the ones who I hurt more than I know, being my self and no one else, whom

Respect for is more than granted – these beings of blood who encouraged me to

find myself, I accomplished this, but some of them still cannot deal with
the fact of the matter I am of no christ, a marijuana smoker, and identify with a class viewed as deviant to the majority, and a writer of poems like these…

Who can't comprehend the poem as a means to relive the darkness of the past and

let it go, in a sense, but always remember what one learned from it…
Or that each day is a learning experience, everything is of value and that to this philosophy to my life I hold,

a value so high, and respect for me like I never had… they wonder why I say some things I say, or why I get depressed at times, how I can live with myself. I do not try to answer them any longer – because my view remains – no one can ever understand

anyone else. But I have connection with my family, and I love them more than I have anyone, and place more value on time spent together – than most aspects of my day to day life itself.

The ones who helped me get through the trip which was the public high school, funny thing, I had one friend who was more like a body guard and a prescription doctor, but I had teachers who were very nice and tried to help me out –Especially Mr. Jones… but these years were a trip through hell but I think they helped me in my formation of my philosophies. Mr. Jones – the only class I think I valued for what it was… I didn't hate myself there, the punk kids hated me, but I just did not care, another good lesson in work ethic.

The ones who seemed on an even keel – smoking blunts in Prospect Park while
contemplating Kafka with gangsta rap pounding on stereo, while dancing rhythm less but in tune for college honor roll.

The ones who are around in the grocery store I work at…
a lot of kids who are just messed up and stupid, some who are really
smart, some older folks who have 20 years there and fit the clerk stereotype to a point that it makes me wanna puke, and some who are there,
and there because it happened, and are alright cause' they just take it for what it is – a job that provides, but can be a pain in the ass, but remain because in a sense –
it is a job. To me – it may be a job – but it's a paycheck. I guess I'm self-righteous – because I don't consider what I do there work, and really don't consider any job there work, managerial ones either… it may be tiring sometimes – but it is a food mart – and makes no difference to anyone besides milk/condoms/Brunswager. But a lot of good employees there, good people, many friends, but I have to do more.

4.

The country where the Mason-Dixon Line cuts through, the survivalists that can make it better for someone, the ones who **scream**, the ones who dream, the ones who learn, the ones who scheme – to get by – factors of reality set in for us – but we know our lives are full because the dream of America may defile itself as it changes daily – but it is heaven. Seems like people in Pittsburgh – take it; break it in their own ways. Agents who either get out but remain in this city, or PA – or the people who don't – but make it by taking it by taking it and making it in their own way, and they break it because they survive the cops, the systems, the laws, the politics, the wrong way right or left way up. Yes, too often they get on one side instead of the idea of what needs to be done and done right, but the point is, they do more than merely get by – they **SURVIVE**!!!

Sometimes it is valuable to **SCREAM** why you **SCREAM** about life – Sometimes it is the only way to get through it…
And it always gets through when you **SCREAM** about the time of your life…
I guess it's only American I got so much crap in my head, on my inside…
I guess I'm some kind of Pittsburgher – because I **SCREAM** like a banshee about it and my city pride.

And I guess I'm not that wrong about my little issues, tonight, tonight. – And I

Think concept is the food for experience; I may be cursed by my mind –

But I turned the curse to my benefit – and realization the most is gained from love and pain, loneliness, pride, everything has value when took with the beautiful challenge mark translated as 1 word – **ACCEPTANCE**.

And there are many good folks out there – **end line 1:** – I have a lot of them in my life – **end line 2:** – Living teaches – give of yourself to yourself and your left, live forever as you were here once – if you lived in America – you were lucky and went for a hell of a ride, because no chance of expression is wasted, meaning possibility can be tasted, and we are here, let's make it, let's stop breaking it. **(end)**.
June 11, 2010 (6:19 am) (I am now 29).

VOW OF FOCUS

Nope… never looked at her that way, sir.
I can see she is wearing a ring, and you know,
… *(cough)*… I consider marriage a, well, I cons-
der marriage one of the most *uhhh*… sacred,
sacred institutions of man… she does have beauty,
but I respect, RESPECT, hear me? I respect the
the vow she took, and I love her, I love her –
so I love her vow – no I have no desire for that
kind of thing for me, or more aptly, not to get on
some half righteous self pity trip – I am likely
not a worthy suitor for any woman – but I was not
picturing her perfect fingers fondling me and

suckling her voluptuous collar bone – I mean no harm,
I am not a threat to your possession of wife – I like her,
and I love her – but I am not a threat to your marriage –
but I do like to consider myself a threat to the "nor-
mal" ways of life communities try to project… I have
to – I have to keep real – and I can – because I know
I will never have a beauteous woman such as your wife upon me.
So I just gotta keep it real, *homey*.
If that fists descends upon me, prepare, prepare…
I will bring my threat to you, but in a way that I don't prefer – I'll jam my thumbs
in your eyes, then I will hit and hit you, *MAAN*, I will hit, I may lose the
fight, but I will hit you, and you will hurt .

PRODUCTIVE PARANOIA
Little did I know, my poop was being saved from my toilet by the government,
to be dissected to find out where I live. I bet you thought nobody dissected poop.
My small hovel is wire tapped – I have known this for sometime,
my telephone as well, there's nothing I can do about it – I rip out the taps and they
reappear the next time I go somewhere.
There are cameras in the eyes of a Marilyn Monroe painting I have above my couch –
and I won't rip them out and destroy a totally attractive, and not that cheap of a picture…
Plus I am not one for taking apart the face of a woman – it would cause even worse dreams than I already have.
I have a computerized recorder in my throat which transmits everything I say into
an office of the CIA.

The government has tried reading my thoughts – they can do that, you know…
but I caused the machines to breakdown within a half hours time…
I know this because I received a mysterious bill in the mail that stated in bold letters –
PAYMENT OF THIS BILL IS MANDATORY: OR ELSE YOU ARE GOING TO THE POKEY.

I paid it… because I will not be subdued that easily. They can try to, though

—
but they won't. Wasn't cheap either.

I can deal with my cameras and internal recording devices. It's kinda funny in a way,
that they could not handle my head... I guess they are just playing a waiting game –
thinking I'll do something, eventually in my place... but I won't be that obvious.

I will keep to my guns, and destroy their ideas with my delirium, however contained to myself or
"peaceful" it has to be, but I'll get by, and die with my freedom,
They can try – but they will never do much to taint me, or destroy the trip of the beauty
I find in life, well, most life.
The government by the year 2043 will find a way to sanction beauty – and probably
everything else... who cares? They are gonna be out of a lot of money if they try
to read the thoughts of everyone – because although there will never be as a destructive
subject as me – there's a' gonna be a lot of malfunctions, maybe explosions or some type
of destructive element on these
machines of thought-reading, obviously, my dear.

9/11/01 For A Mother
Scrumpled up into tiny little balls of paper, she violently threw each piece of the newspaper all over her apartment.
She was crying, not really – tears were rolling down her cheeks though, melting the rouge which she applied very, very lightly, so it was basically unseen anyway.
She was not heaving, though, nor were her lips quivering – quite the contrary – they were pursed tightly, if it were not for the knowledge of the nature of the mouth's place on the face, you might not know they were even there.

But tears fell from her eyes... she knew they were only natural, but it was a long time since this happened, maybe since she gave her kid to people she didn't know in the spring of 1981, even though he went to a good place, it was not with her... so this was the last time she cried, she thought.

But she couldn't distract herself with memory for too long, even though she wanted to – today's horror will be felt for a generation in America, and taught for those generations after – but it was only eventual – but it was still like a life inside her ended today – she did not think of the fact that so many others felt the same way – like something changed into death in the U.S A. .... yes it was only eventual – but it wasn't supposed to happen here.

Her lips were quivering now a bit, she did not heave, but she cried silently hunched over in her chair.

She hoped wherever her kid was now, he could deal with it as peaceably as she.

He dealt with it like he knew how, his parents dealt with it similarly...

He was peaceful, but he cried.
He cried.

BUZZ BUZZ
Written by No-D
In the glory of a unique sky blue eyes of a kitten,
seems like something is there.
The eyes of the beagles all look the same, to me, friendly.
But they seem to hold a pillar of emotion as purely a physicality.
Watching a yellow jacket land near me, another on me, one at my foot,
one on my knee, not stinging... yellow jackets seem to know more than any canine
 kitten critter, yellow jackets know from birth – when they have to die.

But it is summer, so it is not yet time for them, yellow jackets on my foot and knee.
I remain still. I have no wish to kill them...
They know their time – why should I quicken it? They stayed on my body at least four or five minutes.
And I was still, gazing, they didn't seem to mind my watching them.
I think they were flirting, in a sense, sizing, readying their eventual reproduction with each other.
They knew of breeding – nature prominent – undivisive with no sentiment.

And they knew, I knew they knew, that they knew of their short lives, and that
they were going to die in the not too distant future.
They knew their children (their eggs) also would die very soon, too.
The life of the yellow-jacket is extremely brief, and they live to reproduce, and survive the more prominent human species. They do not sting us, unless they need to.
But these bees upon me – they did not sting me, they made love with antenna eyes, the
briefness of their lives was ignored, their mission was the matter.

I lit a cigarette and they flew away, I was becoming uncomfortable
with them sitting there – part of my homo sapien   again…

I hope they were not scared, buzz, buzz.
I found this event beautiful, and inspiring –
like a note of Coltrane…

Ability proves itself before necessity…
Choice is eminent, and one can find appreciation at odd times.

These insects had the ability to sting, but they didn't.
If I would have moved, would I have been stung?

I prefer to think these creatures would not have.
And I am of insect royalty, but they might have had I moved.

But I chose not to… I felt it not necessity.
When these creatures die, I hope they have a
form of insect pride – they are deserving.

The art of necessity –
the necessity to be, and continuance in a life of forever grace…
which brought their ability to keep it cool,

and not sting me, necessity to live until September's wake…
This was a love poem of respect for nature,
a romantic semblance of thought – to a life form

the people of this earth – all should hold to a more respectable delight.

LEIGANCE TO MY LOVED AMERICAN NIGHT:
Written in a No-D mind
Spent too long packing lunchmeat from 2:30 pm until 8. Jimmied my way to pad in a prospect of panorama. Direct hit of resin from my marijuana bowl, decide on writing a Leigance to the night of this time, my prospect of the perfect American night:

Give the Siamese cats a pet, they are stray Siamese cats, who have no home and live on scraps people give them, as well as their lucky heart of nature – that we humans can not tramp, but try – the will to kill the dream of a non-hunted rodent life – to kill that dream with a lunge snap to the neck – the feast of their hunting mind must eat – mind for meat – survival in the blood – hunt for life's ride – live never die and only we can know they can…
I have observed the hunt – and witness on my way in, gutted pigeons – the cat is strength – the cat is the model, the most natural – in the world of animal perspective.

And I saw them tonight, I hit my place – and feel like something happened – like an allegiance of what is – but though I recognize the feeling –
It has forced my gaseous mind to define it as indefinable…   *And this was a quick nic on the mic about it.*

REVERENCE
Written in a No-D mind
I am the devil. I am the Antichrist, on second thought.
I realize quite plainly I am like you, human
            filled plenty with qualities of pain , and inner malice.
But I am the devil, I am like you – I am human… but I *am* the Antichrist.
I enjoy talking with so many – that are not conscious of this blessing upon us.
And you can tell, beneath their fronts of "normal"… they are in so much pain hidden.
This personage is not false; I know. I deal with so much pain indescribable, a pain –
which if given – these people would want to cease their existence …
or find the way of insolent indifference in the weak trip out – suicide, or intoxication which will eventualize into a darker world in themselves.
Simply because they could not take the trip of being human – though they try and
try – acceptance of themselves as the highest animal with a pride to hold high is not found or
sound by them in their time –

they are human – and they are the deviless angeless godless gods/goddesses
of time –

> But they deny their holy presence –
> of a deviless/godless/presence/prince/princesses
> Alive as the balance of truth – the balance
> in time – the balance unthought-of.
> the balance of Every Being Meant for
> the heaven of no sound – the Hell of peace's
> echo within themselves…

The fact that human is the way we roll, so it is the way to roll – We are God
and Satan – we are our death –
so many of the humans are blessed and realize it – but the majority despises
the belief –
In reality – they just can not accept it – and die within their pain – and take
no pride in power in the poem of life…

> And will not even try to accept it.

And this was a quick nic on the mic about it.

YOU ARE I AM
WE ARE
LOVE
HATE
CURCULATION
RECONCILIATION
DAMNATION
BLISS
NOTHINGNESS
BEAUTY
WE ARE HERE

SOLDIER

*The realization of too many brave kids, who thought the military, would
help them be…*
When it makes the most, and breaks the host with a
*Torture of the torture of war… the pungent stain of an undeserved
memory.*
Grab the killer; he is fast as a bullet.
Running forth, dragging the trail of
the freedom of a hapless man put to the
test for his love for his land, so really –

all we can do is let him run, run, and hope
in our brains of meticulous common sense –
he won't get his self killed, and will come back
from the plains of Afghanistan, the sands of Iraq…
and hope he can live without the nightmare of his
deeds – his was justified by the power's lead –
our hope he will not each time he looks at our flag –
break out in a cold, cold, sweat.
But we all know beauty will not be the same for him ever again.

**MY JOB *a thought's reoccurring presence
(a sudden urge for a vain attempt at minimalism)**
Slap me/
Then caress my neck.
You have beautiful
fingers.

I want to hold
them. I want to hold you. I would love
to. It would indeed,

increase the
beauty you bring
into the air of an open

love in an
unappreciated crime of the
pride of an uncommonality nowhere league… or

our jobs
in this common food chain.

NOT AGAIN!!!
Dreamed of us in New York City.
Or France, San Fran – and way,
way a long, long time ago – I wanted to
meet you in the Marines –
Circumstances of me and my insanity,
drinking, and finding ways to escape
to space – such as a week without sleep –
crapped up this dream, and I got shot and
was afraid of being shot again for years, a long time ago –

so long ago I give the "bang" of these former ideas,
or the literal "bullet" absolutely
no credence any more.

But modernity changed so many of
us – I MAY not be trying to dent a pop
can with the candle wick of love's dream –
because so many of us get hit by shit anymore –
either we hit ourselves, or someone else does –
"Hit with Life" – has amended to others like
me. And "Seen too Much"
has become a preference for a loving
commonality… this can happen – but to
me it seems that people (as a generality)…
learn me and force away – or don't "get" my words, at all because of a
"physical" "oddity."

This is the way I see it –
This is what's happened to you and me,
I believe. We really should try our best
to learn to get around that.
Are you listening?
We should learn and find one another.
And bludgeon our loneliness to death without conceit.
We would find we could deal with
ourselves like a dream, if we might meet.
This dream somehow eats my brain, still.
Love is still hard. Though it has changed from a state of its former
place…

Of mundane charisma to a mundane personal uncommonality.
Still in an old jail police state.
Our worlds have been infected, and that means
so have we.
You and me kind of fit…
but not with totality. This is good.
Bring me to your power –
Love can be genuine – *I think*,
and put a mark in the black granite-
stone of both of our lonely realities,
I am a passer by who takes what he can from the passings,
You remain my depth, my other – my Ms. Mystery.

SENTENCING OF HE BY I, MY, and ME
LOOK OUT!!!

We are coming, we will infiltrate your lost cause of false inequitable growth, trust us, quite simply, I and Me are coming forth to destroy what I knows he stands for. All he can do is blush and accept the world's placing of him, I will destroy him in with an honesty in I's deviancy that is so shocking to him, his eyes will widen so wide, I's moonlight will burn into his brain, this is the time for it, if there was any. I and he, the eye of I and my own will destroy his weakness that, though the American Pittsburgh public view as a deviancy, it is his sense of a pungent censor to himself. I has the proper reign of common sense of placating uniquity and realistic heavenly, or hellish divinity, to destroy his eye of falsified logistics, he walks, does not have the energy to run, but he walks and somehow gets away from earthtime reality. More exactly – he WALKED – and divided himself with earthtime reality. Never realizing peaches were bitter green-sour on the other side, still believes the tap water of the spring of worldly sensibility. I dispels him with his moonlight in this hour of the clock's time. I's fruit – O, it not sweet… but it isn't soured with his personal falsity.

I's mind has two eyes, I and Me, are both focused on survival… and I can learn, get by without trying to sanction the unbelievability him (he). I shoots the moonlight death on his eye of he. I needed he for a long time – but sentenced him to burn from the shot of death he was keeping isolated and hidden for so long, I sentences he to feel the pinch – his guilt is so obvious – there is no need for an internal sense of judicial hearing…

It will be a slow death, but he will die, no worries there, chief.

Revolution described. I will die, but not before, not a long, long time after –

He burns he upon I's cross of lethal injection internal delivery of realization.

This sentence was ordained by The Chief of Survival.
    Chief Me.

PSYCHOANALYTIC FINDINGS ON GEOFF

Sunk out of transparency, even. Right now Geoff does not feel like anything, but has a tough time finding content in his sudden form of isolated self.

Maybe just the things Geoff has taken as belief about the world and his place in the world are becoming truer, to such a point that it hurts, it is something that has happened in the recent past as well, and it always takes a lot to find wealth in the pain… but it seems especially hard this morning.

But he knows he will benefit from it, eventually, as pain has always proven the seed of the most honest experience for learning that is, as well as the only true feeling Geoff feels in the world.

Geoff has known a lot of things besides this feeling in the world, but feelings such as love or friendship seem always to have a sharper negative edge of suffering as well as a tone of pain Geoff can not handle, but does: seemingly every night such as last… and he sleeps little on these nights per week, and awakes in hurt,.

As the day progresses, and he sees people he likes at his little occupation which he has a hard time considering work at the food mart chain where he is employed/implied, but there are many people there he likes who help him fade from himself. He puts up a semi-good front of someone possessed by the least beautiful most commonly metaphorical form these others would imply dark with, either sane, or his friends, only a "little" insane. He fronts this semi-well, and has come to the point in his life where he believes he can fake like a firm rubber rake, so can carry on a good conversation with them. It does not mean he is enamored or even remotely likes all of them there… and it does not mean Geoff considers their jobs of any real point of accomplishment… but he realizes many of them are just there for the money, not as a life, and respects this philosophy…and likes them.

But they are not his friends… maybe he wishes they were, maybe he needs to get out more. He hopes it is his experience and that alone which causes him to doubt that so many are worth a damn. He likes many, but it seems he can never find someone real to be friends with, or the seemingly more lost, and so much more desperate impossibility of someone to love, this hurts him the most nowadays. Most of the time, his love and respect for women is stronger than his ability to tell them how he wants very much to have someone, as well as their all consumptive beauty in form beyond physical, but related… these desperate views hurt him too, he still wishes nothing more than to see more of them though, at the same time. Every day the thoughts haunt his mind and he knows it shows. He is not one who takes personal benefit from pity, but he would be willing to accept it if it turned him inside the privacy of a woman, physically or the shimmer of a kind eye and unique mind.

ANALYSIS OF MY JOB CONDITION:
E A T

My Piss-Factory

It pains me substantially that you have to eat. It also pains me that I have to eat, that I have this resemblance to you. I know humans are not the only living forms that have to eat… but it seems troubling to me that so much of this act is done as an act of socializing.

This is why I have an undying respect for dead people and rocks.

It pains me that I am important to you in my place where I am employed, because I am part of the fact that I (in a sense) am a provider of food for you, and you seem to have the little pride of criticizing me, and the job I do for you providing the mortal supplement that is necessary for survival I wish we could do without… no matter how it is packaged or how thinly it is cut, or even if it was not cut – the point is, unless I inject it with my ever growing collection of diseases – it remains sustenance and does the job it is required to, and ends your need of food.

It pains me that there is so much preference for certain food over other food in this country… Some things people do not enjoy eating, I can accept this because my opinion on tomatoes is like eating guts, and have many texture issues that seem to make a lot of food basically impossible for me to eat, partly because the stupid flavor companies invented jarred olives in Italy. Stupid, stupid pickled product to me if I believed evil was brought to earth through the Italians, olives would have essential adage to the evil. But it also pains me that there are so many different kinds of the same thing and all the companies make millions of dollars selling the same thing – because some people prefer certain kinds over others because of the taste. These people use the word prefer a lot when describing food because they think it sounds really fucking fancy, and many people say they won't touch another brand because though they like the same exact thing, but the brand they do not prefer does not satisfy them. When, in reality, it satisfies them just as completely, but they can not accept the fact it does its job of filling their hunger. I don't care, and believe many people would benefit from the fact that if it is not something that repels them completely… it will fill your belly. I would survive on Pall Malls and fish food if I could. But the world of food is so sad because it *is* a world in this human reality. It's only slightly less unreliable than if suddenly each person thought really hard about what kind of plastic paper clips to indulge their office costs in… I really, am not trying to start you on that, but the sentiment remains – cola, pepper, rubber or elastic – my god – who CARES? Why do you do this to yourself?

In fact I think it would be great if food never was given taste, that would have been so much easier, as well as eliminated the idiotic fact that this country is basically driven by the food business, and solidify the idea that not one bit of it really matters or effects anything that happens, I would not have the job I do now, but I would have an employment which is a good one, and so much more productive in comparison, that the mart would seem necessarily nil.

—

It pains me that part of my training is a necessarily vocally trained – well deary, there is not much you can do besides write a letter to the service desk – so, I believe it is my time to bid you a fond adieu and tell you in the proper tone – ahem-have a good day… but this pain can mainly be proudly laughed at because I know I am miles in front of you sad people on the learned life's way – sometimes younger, which bugs the shit out of me and my placing of prominence towards the future as well as my generation, but most times they are older, and I can find worthlessness and modern idiocy's beginning – in philosophic terms. These people are breeding. I have a personal promise to myself to never become one of them – the terminal fools!

It pains me I had a dream years ago, a productive dream to get me away from the mart, but when I had to take math and failed I quit, programming a frustrated envelope opening in me of finding acceptance and never leaving the stanched cutting board for the rest of my life, and only to burn in the fecality 8 years later – a paper burnt to flames – and leaves its shitty sense to self-critical stinky memory. It also pains me that it will be at least six more years of this condoned mask before I can get out. Baby, I got time… but I have a higher notion of self and will to action at this point – my mind isn't at this point in the present. I can distract myself with the music in my head, and so many of the fellow-lost-realized-paths of being there, these women have the highest mark of a weathered energetic natural sense of washed and lived desire by me, my coworkers, but they are basically just either too retarded to think about these things, or more respectably – put themselves so far above the stupid reality of the joint within the mart, not even its mist drifts into their well shaped noses. These are the people I like.

I was standing one day, and a very beautiful woman who I talk to did not give a drunk man the price he wanted – so he told her she was the reason he was going home, strangling his dog, and shooting his wife… after he left, she rolled her eyes, she likes dogs. I said "Well, I'm sure he was a good dog." And the rest of my day was spent remembering this drunk and laughing to myself about him.

I have nothing but value for the initiative provisions my piss-factory provides, money wise I gotta do what I gotta do, and these assholes can be funnier than Dave Letterman if perceived in the correct way. Maybe I'm kind of burned out, but I have to think of something while I'm fulfilling my little pay job – and only let myself cry for this lost decade of my life while on my coffee-smoke breaks. I can't control it, this happens every day. No one is a true connection there, and NONE of them, even my friends would know how to take me if I presented an honest view of myself, and especially not my power hungry bosses whose only power is in the lifetime spent on the piss stained tiled floors, a lifetime spent on a losing mission – there longer than I, toy baby-dolls of false existence, so if they are still there when I split, if I split, I'll spit in their eyes… \

Each day when I sat on my breaks outside, I cried, but only sometimes nowadays.

ANALYSIS OF THOUGHT PROCESS:
SUBLIMINALLY POSITIVE WORD DANCE…

but only if this is what one makes it
Written in a No-D mind

I can't die without crying at least 130 times before the end of the year, it would feel so, like totally, *mondo-retrievioso-humanoido-burnt-lost-know-eeing.*

I am aware I am probably just making this statement up – but when I hurt nowadays I don't get drunk, I don't have anyone to listen to me and even try to grasp my life valuing philosophy stated in psychotic-rambling screams, and I do not punch rocks or bite my nose for physical pain kick anymore, and I feel my past is that, but a generative discipline…

But I did the things I did, and I hurt when I think about them and how they devalue me in your eyes. I cry, but I will never give a thought to killing myself and am sickened by the idea – so the pain has to go somewhere – and not being afraid to cry over the life I learned is the brief release I have to do right now. The pain has to go somewhere. Tears are harmless enough – and help me deal with the life of philosophy I ponder – and this notion as of this date – lets me live and love it with chance –

It does not belittle me that the tears come round less often than they used to –

but I feel like a winner, more than like a team member trading self.

And this was a quick nic on the mic about it.

PATS TO DA' BOOMIN VOICE OF RELIGIOUS THOUGHT
Written by No-D
HEY!!! J=LIKENESS WITH THE CAN DO POWER BLASTING
GENUINE CREEPING LIGHT OF **GOD**. Hey, killer, how would you like
to shoot Indians riding on my voluptuous eyes of the devil continuances
who **POWA**! digs Los Angeles is lost angeless paving the way of cement
descent, believe this idea of having others like it/believe your front
maintenance.
Preface upon the self that reaches to the eternal sky of sea depth in the
penny, no gold in heaven.

ANALYSIS OF SHITTLE
Grains of sand in the dark of discipline…
but not in the commonest self/
Grab time and break its rest.
Think not of biding your time,
but configuring its need with earth,
and tasks to complete, dream of reliance,

Dream the dream of shittle marks.
Or a commonality dream related to having
shittle stains in your pants, dreams are becoming an
earthshaking realization
people die earlier when they don't sleep,

But loss of notion except upon udder need is proof they got off
the cow's milk that will remain when needed.
But at least provides an attraction to the lifetime of energy in nature –
But only then will they have to nightly suckle the teat of sleep.

MY LAST TIME, 4 YEARS AGO AT ANDY WARHOL'S GRAVE
Two times I looked down and studied the grave that held a kind of
movement of emotion for me. I only looked down twice, but the emotion
of my natured and nurtured multiple personage in self of emotion, it keeps
going to this day, because I looked down twice the last two hundred times
past at this grave, but I knew this would be my last visit for a long, long
time… which is why these gazes meant so damn much. I never met this
man, and was about six years old the day he died. His time in this life
only was given a credence of his inspiration that he had in his life, long
after the fact of its course by me… and I am not upset that our paths never
crossed in the literal sense, because his art, his deviled work of a life's
contradiction, is more than a realistic recompense to my knowledge of a

life well formulated, and his glorious legend of being born in the same city as me, as well as being buried right down the street, well that's all I need for a respect which will never die, the art is more important than morality, plus, he lived for making his originality a member of his mortality, and since that it what I see of him, I am in the sense of an average guy's perception of the life he made for himself. Many dismissed it when it was there, many still, but if he saw me – I would be the perfect consumer of his work and life, because I gather my impressions from his mark on art and a life of media-pop and odd, and that is how his perfect "disciple" can take him – as a consumer fascinated by these traits.

It fades at times, but is always there, because his token outlook was form in portrayal, it is always there, and to learn from EVERYONE is the notion I admire most in his questionable entity, not hero. But a sharp insight of what you can do if you put your mind into a unique abstraction of art which is beautiful for what it is, it is life... and its outlets for you are indispensable.

So, I eat lunch with my Dear Mother, and my dear Aunt Butchy (who I call Honk), and we know where we are going. These two ladies do not enjoy this fate of necessary destination, but in that respect I, this "child" was always spoiled, and it did not cost any money, so they took me down there, no problem. I was in the cemetery, and I only looked at the actual grave twice, but I took more in from this last visit for a long time than I ever had in my many previous ones. My eyes wandered to the other marble shapes of eventuality, to the ground, saw a beetle, might have been a roach and I let him live, maybe he had a piece of this legend beyond legend in my eyes in his insect belly. I knew this was my last time here for a while. I would not come back until I got some serious writing done, may not be good, but I needed to view this task as my honest work in life, and not come back to this subjective sight until I took the piece of work in creation ethic from the Andy life that was, took too young, and live for this ethic of bettering myself through work ethic, my own definitely, but these two glimpses at this grave which bore the artist's name instead of his name in actuality, inspired me to do this and I think to a point, I have. I think I have improved in what I do based on my time and ethic for work and necessity to provide inspiration as well as human-necessity to get by and make and create in the dark semblances of my time which seem to have been forced upon me, and my notion to get them out in an insultingly, yet honest and hopefully productive time in being. I'm not done yet. Publication will be celebrated by a return to this simple, typical, gravesite of a truly driven and rewarded being. It is a pact I took with him.

If I were to believe in a faith, I would say my faith for initial inspiration for my want to create came from Andy… a teacher, a seeker, who made who he was, and had not a single bone about seeing the interior of love for his time here, and had not a bone of repercussive thought for his life in a field he defined, and made his, lived it like a nature because its nature was his, and his legend… and there will never be another one.

I AM NOT YOU'RE/YOUR ENEMY

I am not you're enemy. I really laugh at the dead idea of comparing myself to Warhol, but he seemed to live the perfect American dream, like I say, to give one's own work merit is to accept benign falsity, which I did in the previous entry regrettably. I am not you're enemy. I don't really want to hurt people; I really do not even want to disturb them unless they need to be. You have my most extreme devotion for saying a lot of it isn't bad, and it was kind of nice to finally meet someone who realized, I don't want to be an enemy, but to credit them with their defilement of the America we love, or adhere to, in our scent of the smog with children in it floating above our enemy, the smog is the dark beauty of a system of willful words, from the life we birth, the hope to give something to the children floating in the smog to help them find the power in themselves, and rise above the place this country is at and is headed. The enemy is the water in the lake, sewage mixed with fungi that we hope they can defy the obstructive gravity of which pushes them into drowning in the lake. Water falling is the enemy, and the justice in the smog is the erudite to its misty yet sharp edge.

I am not. I am not. I am not your enemy. Don't make me say it. I can't. I don't want to be your enemy, and I am not your enemy, but I seem to become to each person who ever knew me an enemy, eventually. But a few have bounced to me again, only a few. And it does not bother me losing respect in many of their eyes. But I don't want to do that to you, so I won't.

This was a piece of word jumble, from someone who isn't anyone's enemy, because he does not have anybody that he matters a drop of evaporation to.

JULY 4, 2010

Remember that time, in the afternoon, right when we were going down to *Eide's*, to get some old-school punk on vinyl, and we indiscreetly fucked each other good on the bus?

I remember I was extremely excited and feeling especially sexual and patriotic, it was the fourth of July in 2010. I knew I had to have you, on the bus, on the bus, and you were not hard to convince to make love to me there, because we are both a lot alike in that respect, we dine on weird experiences such as making fun of people that are jogging at The Point in the center of Pittsburgh, and having sex on the bus... plus its weird, on days like Memorial Day or the Fourth of July, we feel especially diggin of the country even though we spend hours upon hours displaying our dislike for it's politics and O so many of its systems on normal days like May 11 or December 25.

People I know, which are few, but they think I am pretty weird for the things I say about you... they do not think you are the vision of beauty that I do, they have a hard time maintaining a conversation with you about me, they don't think you are anyone special or that we're gonna last, because they have the idea of me, from spending almost as many long nights with me as you, that you are too typical for me, and someday soon I will break into the outlook on life which life has taught me, or tell you one of the things life did to me or I did to me, break down and make you run away. They do not know I told you more than I ever told them, and have let you know more than anyone, even my mother or analyst. You do not like them very much, you view them as unproductive and lazy people who smoke marijuana and do not see the proper benefits... basically drunkards after a joint. Plus, you view them as stupid. I do not think they are stupid, but agree with the former point, and I love you because I have finally connected with a woman on so many facets involved in the life trip.

You have a son, and you have a boyfriend who is so typical it is basically an insult to yourself and your depth as a woman to go out with him, the kind of man who gets drunk and goes to Steelers games.

But this July 4, 2010, you let him go, and you say you want to start going out with me, and stop poisoning your son's mind with this selfish person, and you would like me to, in a loose sense, start being with you as well as him as often as possible. You look divine on the bus, as we ride, as we ride. I take in each freckle on your body, as we copulate on the bus, on the bus, as a more divine work of art than a painting by Van Gogh, or a poem by Ginsberg. We are one on the bus, on the bus. We disconnect from the world and the privacy of the act, we just do not care, our patriotism driven sexuality makes us become one, and I notice I love you, but do not say it directly, and you love me.

We are made to leave the bus, it's a long walk home, and we do not care. You are a vision and love me; no one else knows you, or me. We walk and share many feelings. I am someone and you are someone and together, at least for a time, we provide life with a fact of infinity upon the mask of commonality.

We are **one, we** are **lone, we rode** the **bus** and didn't need to guard ourselves, **on this lone,** *together* **American night.**
(Sunday, July 04, 2010)

THINKS
Cremation into dust, how I would dig forever.
Burned and lit my days and nights through life,
noticed how when the time dies down, and the
flaming gibberings turn to ash on the cement ground –
they are the flesh of peace, flesh deceased, remembered
by no one… except me. It would be nice to be a burnt heir
of nothing but… nothing but… a notion of time spent, of peace.

Fading in death, but the idea someone can recall my dream
of being, someone may possibly remember me.

But I have some life to live, some dreams to fulfill until,
so I don't need to think about death yet…

Dreams of life conclude and cease the thievery of it.
Death is permanent, make life your spin, produce and make do,

And the essence and value in life can turn death into
the realm of the end, but living at your most accelerated –
is a joy in a lifetime, a darkness sigil, yet value in light's illumination.
We are here; we are the division between, a lifelong suicide, no matter the
life lived.

Not even thinking of death, dreams of power in the self…
Forever as the silver fishes in the stream of the acceptance of
ourselves as being because we got here =

Worship time lost as well as born. Worship inevitability.

We are here, and we are now, we light life's dark road…
We are here, we can see, we can learn the challenge of an existentialist
peace.

TO BE SAID IN A RITUAL

Deliver the rapture of Hell – the ecstasies – the beauty in the darkness in the literal hell

of yourself – the mind of your self. Just as the wine of forever, the primal

life savage who beat it, the heir is the darkness as beauty...

The heir will be a princess, and her loveless

indifference but with a tone much like the divi-sion

in a mortal man. And the coming of nothing...

The black nightresses of themselves/

Respect her – her kiss will not be short –

her tongue leaves itself in the growing population of the willingness towards what is, and

she has eyes – and beautiful dark jagged but polished body of...

PERFECTION!!!... those of us who know this depth in blackness DO NOT SEE THIS PERFECTION in our minds...

but we know this opulent beauty in darkness is there, but we take

our life as a GOD, the time of the self, never to return –

the dream of life is the dark, and accepting it. The depth, the work, the doing as the moment   progresses, taking it as it comes,

dine on the beauty in the sense

of depth in   creation...

<u>WE ARE HERE</u> – <u>WE ARE HUMAN</u> – <u>WE ARE GODS</u> – <u>WE ARE</u>
DEVILS
WE ARE!

ELDERLY IRISH FAIRY WHO PLAYS THE ROLE GRANDFATHER
Hey slinger, hey bubba, hey booboo come to PAPPAP Geoff and he'll tell you the story – until page 94, he'll check you're mate, and place a crown on your king, he wins,
you will remember the story on May 11th, September 11th, but lad –
YOU WILL HAVE NO MEMORY OF ME, OR WHERE THE LIFE GAME QUOTE CAME FROM BUT YOU WILL LEARN FROM IT. GOODBYE, CHEERIO, AND POINTY TOE.
(I give the boy a kitten, wink, snap my fingers, and vanish into golden

glitter)...
(Into the old man winter wind of forever).

THE GRIM REAPER GANG
Written in a No-D mind
Heh heh, we's about to dive you home, dive you home. You gonna jump, and we's a won't break your fall, but Chili, we most sure something will, but it gonna wrap itself around you, and the fall in motion of here once, get ya in eternal motion and bein nuthin trips you around and everywhere, so's nothing is a different word than something, but so similar, and the nothing trip, was perfect because it been where you lived in... I gotta trip on out, you gonna pounce in the reality of what was, and the space of what is – in the river of eternal nothing... out.
This was YOUR last nic on the mic about it.

TIME IN **MY GHETTO**
Come hither be nither
remain sensual and beautifying.
Blissfully dark in your
passion of the mastery of
the moth-grey finishing brush strokes upon the landscape endeavor.
The landscape of having been, so the landscape of being – forever.

REMEMBER THE TIME (Vampiric Memory)
Have a sample please – we invite you into these texts of uncooked beef.
Slimy with the blood's life-force, we invite you, come closer, closer –
let me caress the sexually uninhibited natural purple polished opulent
throbbing vein to the above left of your collarbone.
I desire this depth, and suckle it. Warm as a hot bath
risen to my tongue, throbbing like a raw flow of wont...
=...
Tch...
Welcome.

CONCEPT OF SPACE VALUE
Simply and inevitably time is space, and space is valuable, as in there is
a space to fulfill in an emptiness waiting to be instilled, a presence in the

reign of nothing that could be seen as the depth of its physicality, and when space is filled– it shall remain with something inhabiting it, over here or there, or if it shan't be filled – it remains – and will remain even after we cease to be. Space is time and space in time – the nothing is as heavenly an unpainted Holden Caulfield mosaic.

NIGHTS AT THE REMAINING, LISTENING BUT NOT HEARING
I.
Did dreams make a sense of lifetime,
beautiful structure, in the acceptance,
(even enjoyment) of a lifetime in hell
or depth of the truly honest divinity which is…
ITSELF.
CHAOS:
REVELATION
SIGHT:
DETERMINATION

The fact of the dark beauty in being in a
state where you can love life
through the fact you are alive,

and god, forever learning. Sometimes still hurting.
Did you ever make the sense of that?
Beautiful dreams and the nightmares of life. Ever seen them as like things?
Can you dig that?

Do you get what I am saying?

THIS
is my most favorite part of my job at the food mart food mart limited.

II.
ALSO
So this kid got a Ramones t on, so I salute his bravery…
Engine died a long time ago, Maggie, she gone too, dead is history. Been.
Born into LIFE: a dry ellipsis, that's
Me. I'm a knight looking in his pony's ass for a piece of carrot.
This is my reference to an ellipse, and my given notion torn towards a personal eclipse.

III.
RANDOM TWILIGHT THOUGHTS OF THE WAY I THINK
A psychoanalysm in verse
RANDOM CONNECTIVE THOUGHTS
1.

Hey! So delayed was our meeting, I almost tried the subway be-
tween the river in Pittsburgh, and the mist of the flickering
fastfast Lincolns racing down Broadway, ha ha but you came and the
density of pale blue eyes held a more intense need for action than a river of
sunlight, or star light on the Passaic.

Have you ever seen that interview show where this was the newscaster
intro-line…
right before they took a break to advertise pastry flavored toothpaste? *"One
scoop will do you fine and white. With sprinkles"*.

Yes, I always really liked certain newscasters, some seem good ones, I
mean –
of course just like the other ones – half of what their echoed breathed voice
says is
more than likely baloney, but the way some female ones pronounce vowels
–
they do it so, smoothly nownownow.

Pine trees fall eventually, many people know this\
I know many lovely pine trees, and I touch every single one I pass, I
caress   each trunk, with their thoughts. I will miss them when I watch
them fall
I share a part tree brain, and I will be notified when each pine
ploots and I will rush to watch, I'll be there quicker than my penny-bus
ticket's echo that is louder upon my coffee stained carpet, than my awoken
downstairs neighbor who screams at
me from the floor at 3am to stop playing death-metal so loud. The Engine
lives.

Were you listening to music, possibly Sgt. Pepper the night this
happened?
Vibes from a life, traced to the penance of the ever so realistic notion to
kill the bad guys, we American folk can do this, we knows time does not
change

or benefit or we can let each of those poopers who shot an officer fry, oh…
yes the man on the left killed two city women, who the judge ruled
wore toomuch   rouge, plus these gals they was Satanists.   In
makin this land like it should be, these hell lip wearin' toe paintin' women,
who/ has no place but in Salem, its okay he got them/he's getting out in ten
to continue
the lord's work, I never said that.

Cop = immediate death penalty no matter circumstances… slaying
someone
the pigs had a problem with because of eyeliner and a mark of Baphomet,
well that's not
a real decision…
***THERE IS NO REASONABLE THOUGHT, NO SENSE OF GOODNESS
OR ANY REALISTIC CLOSURE TO THE VICTIMS IN THE LAW OF
THE DEATH PENALTY. ANYTIME – THE LAW OF BARBARITY.***

2. PSYCHOANALYSM OF A SITUATION OF SOMEONE I WANT
TO KNOW ME
Scattered tattered blinded schemed loving is the time of an eternity, and –
the question is always the same, and I can dig it, I'll let the depth of a sea in
the night ascend on your violently smooth red flaming hair, I never made
a sense of your equation, but I love you, but probably confuse you just the
same. Not many women as divine
as you, are similar to me in the fact we enjoy immensely the puppy chow
we steal
from Snoopy feeding bowls in the city, and place it on a Ritz,
and know the shih-tzu doesn't appreciate its $5.62
flavor of a mush like none other being stolen. Horsemeat sticking between
our incisor teeth.

We do what we have to, to survive the facts put on us by our pasts.

But you will not "have" me, I'm too weird for you – I guess some normal
people just like eating dog food.

Doesn't matter, you are still cool. *What color are his eyes? You can tell
she is a
Wrestler.* This daily customer has requested I wrap her grapes in paper?
I wrap her grapes
in paper, fingering them,
staring at you,

and put on a slightly different version of me and you in a play using
the words thou   and thus many times   sitting on a tree...

I make like a snake – as I play out a semblance of thought eating luscious
grapes,
in a Broadway light my Adam and Eve stricken Bodhi Bleecker fantasy.
This is the semblance of peace I dream walking through the morning to my
vulgar simplicity every Sunday.

3. (Continuance of 2)...
Faces and places show, dreams and reality hilt being one entity. Things
are
realer. But flickering with the light of peace in the dream, to your beauty
in a faith in something of a past time, a past life, remembrances and
accuracy. And deviancies.
That's not how I deal with it, and I do not like it –
but I would never change a single thing about you.
                    You are You, and what you make or choose   to break
divides your naturally dimpled smile
into a state of perfection natural, learned in a life
in the ways of making do in the life, and making it
by surviving it – and this is the power you have,
and I am what you call "blessed" to even the slightest
glance of your eyes, the most beautiful I have ever seen.

Eyes which can live the life,
but keeping a balance of dreaming space at all times. And a life so led
which appreciates the beautiful space in it, like an accuracy of mine.

4. PHILOSOPHY
I mean, this is my view on that: When do people dream? Obviously when
they are asleep, letting the body rest, the learned body, that is. Being the body
people study with the punctuality of cemented reason, is a convenience.
So, the human condition, what we put ourselves through daily, whether it
be construction work or making coins in a cup jingle-jangle, that *requires*
of us. The human condition is to tire ourselves, or <u>work</u>: in a less syllabic
word sense. And every person, makes learning the fact, not act, but fact, of
their lifetime... people know this, cats know this, but not enough people
know it consciously.
What is this that bends? It is your A R M, defined at birth by the need to

know how to mentally phrase your view, your love, your mortal words, and your attitude on life. Therefore – the thirst for knowledge, beyond knowledge, survival, is what we fill ourselves with realizing it or not. The point is – LIFE is in a knowledgeable, functioning quest, we have beautiful eyes, we sense. From the time we are in the womb until the time we have none more on the clock.

Dreams are significant because we infuse our life into them. Even if we do not wish to, we imply the term 'event' into our reality, our selves, and dreaming has no sense of curtailing the subject which one has made, or has been made unto thou. Sometimes it can be fantasy, unbeknownst images, but the essential point I am making is that the mind has a natural skill and shift for symbolism, to make it easier for our bodies to think too much of as the event unfolds in reality. And happiness is a fluid for adrenaline, so good happenings can be exemplified into perfect happenings, events which viewed as perfect by the subject in their flesh and walking self, can be twisted to further ecstasy, possibly remembered and LOVED, to make for a positive outlook in the coming awakening, evolving our place in the world. Bounty, however unaccepted, still flying with angel's wings.

And if we think about them instead of rave about them or try to forget them, we would metaphorically fly. Our wings would grow and our wings as people as we are, the highest species real or faith-based there is – we would be the essences of beauty, all of us, will to have learned, survived, willed, and add more to the earth, and some things will seem a lot more lasting… like our lives, but most importantly, one of the lasting ingredients which is the Love we have, and the Love we bring. Most significantly – *the life which WE live.*

Love CAN be all there is. Our eyes staring toward the depth of the Antarctic notion – but not a grain of thought in not taking our Dreams into our life, because they are the forever feature. It is not impossible for the human to do this. The realization of these thoughts for our provocation on the Depth we all await as our condition animal, but most functional, forever living, therefore never dying, because we never were taught to think of it, what happens does, but we will not even have THAT. We will and live, we will cease to, but disintegrate like a cigarette ash. Pain WOULD be eliminated from the process of death.

Because we are Love, we shall live and learn and love life, like we should.

The previous was the blueprint for the extension of the human species.

IV.
RANDOMIZATION OF FREE FORM EXPULSION
Written in a No-D mind:
What are you, ya **powa** – your fist and your **spliff** your semi-
Trigger pullin index digit, that's you so you's you –
And I'm me in dis little rhyme, listen if you want – or just walk away,
Mind my bass, but mind my retaliation, of the time in a life – as a ski on the
skate, on my time, in these rhymes.

I AM GLAD I WORE MY GLASSES IN COLLEGE THE FIRST TIME
Geoff on the college course he values still:
To my past professor of English 102
I can't get to spinal sense, ear sense, urinary sense, of living and not giving,
I give and I live, and YOU have given me your unique defiance implied if
not willed in learning,
and these are the words of your old narrator. I write about me to learn
                about you, part of me is you… and you are becoming   less of
a 'part,'
but I am not sure if that's how I want it. You were an example of our
species.

But a living digestion I can't fight, which is your elegant mastery of interior,
and the hair of a professor, of English and brings me to the notion that some
things are in a sight – permanent.
You were something, I was in the 9 kids who didn't drop this, and I wish
I could take the English course again… I do not plan on forgetting your
class.

THE MEETING BETWEEN AN ALCOHOLIC BOSS WHO THINKS HE KNOWS THE MAN IS HOOKED ON A SUBSTANCE – THE MAN IS NOT, ONLY HAVING A NERVOUS FIT OF FRUSTRATION IN THE FACT OF HIS POINTLESS OFFICE EMPLOYMENT, HE'D RATHER WORK CLERICAL

Boss No-D to employee #4 Josef Joseph:
Look for the poppies, light the pipe, drink until you die, hey, jim, watch the
red steam of penance on the clock of the digit, becoming more tonal
each day, every day you hit or guzzle, or peak to puke, or pass out and puke
in the morning, but as your employer, I just wanted you to know, I know.
You make it in time you flow the folders unlike any other worker.

                        I just wanted you to know, I know,   and you
will fall, or maybe come to,
               maybe not, just keep your pace proficient, but I know, I
               know. I will not search your desk.

III.

RANDOM ACCENTS OF A MISTY, ETERNALLY HUMAIN BRAIN BEING
WHY CHILDREN HAVE THE MOST HONEST IN CONCEPT OF THIS REALITY
Written from Geoff as well as a child:

Scowl at me, bring me life, have my love, wake me deep, be my wife, we'll make
another's lifetime love. What I say, who I go?
I be the man who is cold as *The Thinker* outside in winter.
I be the woman who has wet dreams about Walt Whitman.

I be the time line of the child, the essence in the ambivalence, because the
life soda that says like it sees, has not caused any acid burps for sayings like
you don't please… I be a beautiful thing.
I will NOT willingly listen to any of you TEACH!!!
(I don't KNOW how YOU work, but it isn't right, I will word this in a
spiff\death/trip\word) (Simply put for the layman – I'm more free than you
because I say it like it is).
        [n' you can't], [gum in your hair]: ☺

Childhood aspect of divinity, why children are stronger than we.

9-11-01

Geoff on his feelings after the attack on New York, Washington, the Shanks
Ville incident and for every life destroyed this day:
City on fire, flaming like blades of light in a sword fight.
Pastry on my breath and gold in my hair, I watch the city burn.
A river in my pants, and the recognizably impossible reaction that –
I need to get them out of there, in my mind. The moment's coma
          reaction did not make me notice I couldn't. But I **NEEDED**
to   **help**   **them.**

ANARCHY

My ears hear thumping of steps, walking towards me and away from me.
I like my interior audio realization of them, like my city and <u>My</u> <u>Ghetto</u>.
Building a stereo better than the most precise in sound which can define
Ravel.
Box of sound made by Sony or another common man-made stereo
company,
Which like my personal stereo was constructed, and at times, still,
performs
like a dream of an unreality. I take pieces from its sound, and the echo of
Ravel,
Lou Reed, or any master of symphonic melody,   always   stays,
progresses in the
events, that shape – hat shape and   make me.

Beauty and perseverance to remain and paste the time of a life inthe power
of the sight of productive anarchy in my self. Music is a justifiable peace,
in many, many ways.

TIME TO DANCE

Your second life, your second life does not permit.
Your second life is the law of the all, the permit is not
a word of existence in your second life, only inside you, and memory
gives the word nothing but a vulgar air when something
of the permit, the law, the pittance of a jagged way in which
the permit you needed was the law of a lifetime you
must not permit in the new law of love in depth.
But in a sense, where you were was necessary –
Rimbaud, Ginsberg, parted the way for you when the
permit was needed –

the Mozart – the Mascis –

all made the way you needed to exist –

made the permits of inspiration you used for the way of the great gathering you used. Sooo many more – we could not count them. And they remain in the echo of a passion which is to keep; you had to buy these amphetamine words which were a power, the **POWA!** to the pride in an existence which is the former you, you learned with pride.

But not to return, the rest of the old life was used – for this is your time FOR

REACTION instead of lost souls, not even The <u>WAY</u> of LaVey, or PATTI SMITH.

They were none more than a shadow for the **NEW WAY, YOUR WAY**. Though they were those who found the dream and knew it in their own way – hah hah hah hah hah = they KNEW this

Necessary DEED of the owing to the blessing that they were here.

And are echoed in the YOU of REACTION, **POWA!** Fate and trying to LOVE the small part remains. BUT NO PERMIT of persecution is needed… come on now –

TIME TO DANCE instead of INGEST, time to make do –

It has come because in the new you will learn the way to do MORE! **POWA**! The crime wins of the way that kills so many with the human spark of human ingenuity

 IN THE FACE!

TIME to SPEAK, my child, make the change we waited so long for in your self.

You are REACTION to injustice, and you use you and you and the people you meet – no longer for expanding them to a love for life – but to make the day reactive.

REALIZATION to your pride of having it in you!

POWA!

Say the words.

Learn the Law.

VOW OF FOCUS SPEEDFAST

Come on man – get in the van…

TO MY PSYCHOTHERAPIST:

Don't tempt me to tell you everything –

'cause you'll break it –

because the **VOW OF FOCUS**

will be explained fast as a lighting flash –

and will burn you – you will be

insulted, demurred, and in less thanthan a heartbeat,

it will make a common sense to you –
and you will understand, and demand and learn –

Me and my way, learn me real,
EXPLANATION will be quick,
and as some form genuinity of learning to

Love the life – LOVE not THEIR way of it – come on.'

Maybe I should tell you, you could know.

Before I tell you I will imply the warning we will soon
be switching chairs... but I KNOW you will see.
But you will be the one on the road to beauty in study of
ACCEPTANCE...

But dig – you will KNOW This WAY of the need to learn to daily/nightly
burn.
– and you will know the understanding of
accepting THIS WAY – hurts and learns – learns to hurt –

never hurting IN learning – and you'll KNOW the way through pain –
you **CAN** become one of **THE WAY** – and you will take to it –
and realize it was always there...

I think you are one of the few front to back brain –
Jims who could get it –
You will open a practice in Tangiers –

and become MORE well known than Freud..

(THERE)!

Come on, man, get in the van – you got to know now – let me finish – get
in the van –
drink a cup of divine tea – and you'll hit the road of
an Honest Eternity –

Or you may recommend I kill myself, *hahaha*
but it won't get through... dig, and I'll be scheduled for a 9am lobotomy,
probably.
But I kind of think you could get it,

but it would take time, and the hour ride would extend you to the timeless
sin of understanding my pride, and I think you could gather
a new way of dissection, possibly, possibly.

Lou, Lou – What's The News?
Come on, come on, come with me, chili. I throw the chili at people I do
hate, whether productively or unproductively in the town of New York
City, man.
I buy two quarts,
It lasts a pretty long time,
I guesses I'm a Pittsburgh chili expelling New York City Man.
(Lou Reed on stereo)

HAIL!
Seminal pressing organize the [Krishna] in the brain dramatization in the
the Satan based pride in human delicacy.

WAIT FOR
Don't try the way to finding out anything
Wait and wait.
Don't ask her for your presence.
If she knows,
she will take it, and a Love will relate
devoid of material pasts, or judgmental states.

JOURNAL I
Hey baby heybaby heybaby heybaby hey baby…
Scales of trumpet upon BREAK IT UP… bread in my belly, STOP IT
or BREAK IT UP – decision of a lifetime, ending but making it until I
no LONGER REMAIN. Until ain't no one heard a damn thing I **SAID**.
Castles in the forest, gold as IN a determined person but *NOT* based on no
publishing write cost, and the babble of a forever teenager, who had not
a book published that was even a considerably nice phrase of verse, and
nothing real but cute but it so sad he is thirty years old.

Who said list?
1. I'm not a floo-floo jerk, angel… and I am not elderly, and neither are
you, and god knows I am not a little kid; I really wish you could see this.

2.There is no longer any oil flowing into the gulf, but the wildlife and the
ocean space infected, shall look at it like the others (humans) relate to the
concentration camps massacre. But it is good it has ended – time for bed,

Kitten.

3. will give you twenty dollar to beat the living crap out of me, so my senses become physically distorted, and I am no longer severely allergic to cats – I would love to have a kitty-cat.

4. Stare at the walls....

II.
Pledge to never Refrain...
The day was July 15, 2010. This was a day this was a day, of the coffee-slightly-a lot of music-a little weed – and the day of my pledge to never refrain... but begin to attack – begin to never rely on the person I was to give me credence for the reason I say some things, or am dead silent through the day even if someone speaks directly to me in this world I am forced to remain– but the marks I made or make of the impression in no longer deserving of the explanation for why I don't seem right, it would waste way too much energy, more than these people deserve, they are all the same, and never would understand it, anyway.
The day was July 15, 2010. This was a day this was a day, of learning more than I ever, ever knew about me. I looked into me, and found things there, I had things unknown happening. What is this sensibility for survival in the need for the others, however distasteful I find the majority of them? But I learned I could find the hint of minority in most of them and respect it. Nobody I have to deal with on any basis remotely affects me in any way besides my parents, right now. The realistic sense of my genuine surviving and defiling my life as a savage inside, and I might as well try, while I am here – to just deal with the ones I differ substantially with, in other words, friends shall remain friends, and enemies will be enemies, the ones who hurt me shall never accomplish recompense. I decided to define my life this day, but only in the futuristic sense. Engine was cool, we had a lot of good times – but Engine is dead – and I can not do a thing about it... My Mother and my Aunt Honk and my brother and my baby cousin remain – but they are really not willing to find the sense in this form of natural being I found – it seems impossible to them, as is true with the most of the world's people.
I defined action as life as to acceptance only to fool the reaction of life, and what it tries to do to me right back in its scenic but shattered undecorated face, but to define my space.
Nothing is permanent, but life as in been here and did it, I saw the ash float
–

In the sense of which I am… my self and the fact my life is forever.
My sense of life in a NEVER REFRAIN, the ash of a forever factory, one
that takes a long time to fade, but benefits, recycles itself in its own unique
way. And my pledge to need the mode of need for more life, and my chance
to still get it!

III
ANOTHER ONE OF THEM

I forgot about the time we were sitting on the bay,
and I got the sense that you were there smiling beside me
I never knew it since, and I won't sit there again
but its good I saw the bay on the lake shores of Japan…

But you smiled a buck-tooth grin, thinking that I was in
your game, you didn't realize all I thought about was how
you were all the same, but you smiled and you knew I was
so good and would remain, have come such a long way, maybe baby, but
I wouldn't tell you how I survived it if you paid –

You thought this way meant an acceptance of life's games…
You asked me what I've done, and if I scored a way to take the shore
of the way that you pertain, as we walked back to the store.
My front was good, I believe, and I said I'd take a piece of our time back
to my Pittsburgh eve.

The front was distinguished and you thought I meant these
things,
you don't deserve to know how I get around in my head,
and this difference makes not a wade of sand, in my time before either you
or me are dead,
and you remain where you never fit in the peace, of a lifetime spent but
forever asleep instead of taking action –

You are dead like all the rest – and you try so hard to always forget –
you will never be seen by me – as besides just another one of them.

IV
INDULGENCE FOR THE DEVIL
Written in a No-D mind

No, no, no. No more potatoes please, stop potato child, I do not want any
more.

He puts more potatoes upon my plate, and smiles his red clown lips
blinking slowly, horns on his head blinking. He giggles and it is the most
evil thing I ever heard.
I mush them in my mouth, they are delicious potatoes – I swallow,
Bring on out the meat, potato devil.

V.

BEAUTY NOTION FROM WHAT I WITNESS
Petals in your depth of crimson hair.
Camouflaged like not a thing
          I ev-
              er saw…
But knew throughout my whole lifetime –
      beauty.

VI

ADMITTANCE I
Moonlight Time
Hep hep… 1234…
Come over here Tricia, be sitting on my lap.
Rub my groin and my arm, since you got the rap.
We been here for 12 years, and I think its time you knew –
who you love and bred is not the man he shows to you.

I'm not gonna rap about some bullshit that I seen…
and I ain't gonna tell you I have eight more kids…
Simply in your terms – I'm from a different place,
a place that shoots down every night, glimmering upon every face.

You can call me moonlight, but I don't really have a name…
and I took my form from shadow – a circumference of the same.
I was loved when I was from the sky, and saw a lot of life…
but when I was in Pittsburgh in about last twelve years ago's time –

You were dancing in my life, I reflected off your thigh,
I reflected off your hair, in your eyes, in your life,
as you swayed in the circle near your cats, in the night.
And I took an offer moonlight gets, to take something out of mortal
flight.

It did not take a lot to turn to my form to love –

the darkness all about you – just as shining from above
and our children will become, and when there done they'll light the eve.
But we have different blood, so you have a decision to receive.

Or a request – a request – Will you come with me?
We can bring the night Our Us – and not have to wear a daylight sleeve...
It is the light of Sir Moon – the peace in taking what will be –
We could lend a piece of who are we. We make to him – and to switch dull
night's life for our light of
A worldly showered gleam.

HAIL WOMAN ENTERNAL REST
Little time does not do much for me to do to save my name, so I will make
it short –
I'm off to bid farewell to this world of hurt, and throw myself off a cliff.
I have a deadly tumor in my uterus, and a worm in my prostrate... and
every time the worm takes a nibble – I feel painful icicles freezing my
spine, the tumor remains there, but all it does is remind of the elegant form
of space and beauty I am about to become –
As One who was with you...

BRIEF NOTION OF RESPECT FOR YOU
Delight in the time, bide the blatant rhyme...
take what you will, but take it all like fine wine, scrape up, polish up –
remember to forget, but remember to learn
so you can be smart when you are dead, and while alive you will powerfully
burn.

JOURNAL II
I.
Crapped up the system crapped up the language crapped up well just about
everything – the politics of the United States are completely demonic...
a term as you may have figured out I give some respect, if you have read
thus far. Politicians are demonic, not only in the suit and tie gaze of most of
them, or they make it easy to think they are like us, regular to our minds of
"good" people, a little stubble or a little bit of sexy cleavage can prove this
to just about any voter... and being in my state of mind regarding politics
and my experience, I learned that they are all gonna have a complete or
mostly complete career of taking us even deeper into our own arrogance
– I learned and most of the time vote this way – though usually the left
have far more type of my guy characteristics, this does not change a bit
that each one of them is destructive... I think its cool, and I listen to them

and like both "parties" ideas, immensely at times, but that's the sense of a demonology I respect, because I know even if I love every aspect of hope that would be accomplished which they say, I know, if they are lucky – maybe ninety-five percent of the things they promise will not happen – and making believable promises takes a skill – and they more than likely get people who do not know this, and two years later these people are crying for the lost place of their country, and shaking their fists violently cursing themselves for their own stupidity in their belief in the things they said would get done, and the polar opposite is happening. So – what the hay? – prefer stubble and the chewing of bubble gum, a flavor you too love – what else do we have to really go on? – because lots of shit will continue to go down – too many times even worse things – but all equal in the horror of a metaphorically religious hell that they propagate... and making Abraham Lincoln a symbol of probably just another one of a them fucking politicians to the majority – instead of the hopeful individual with a hope to maintain the aspect in pride in the time of the beginning time of the greatest human dream – America.

II.

BUDDHISM:

Get with it go to it something insane, forget the time in the grace of a lifetime anomaly. Return, return. Come to some Buddhic refrain. What have you to lose in this same shit different day game? Cloud of smoky air in the face of the race, no matter where you're at you stay in the gentle excessive air of humanity's grace. But Buddha doesn't mind, and will not slap you on the back; Buddha won't be over to have coffee, besides his statue in my lap. He doesn't promise some kind of reuniting phase, but his twinkling eyes made this statement once plainly – and knew he never would again.

He was sitting beneath Bodhi, in my version of the story, and he saw something behind his eyes, like a shapeless circle, a circle without line but a circle in the mind, the circle in the ride, the circle in the diamond and the circle of resign, and the outcome is as great as the clean air around in his vision, and after he died, he saw the circle seamed, possibly in the air he became, or possibly in a life lived complete – and now he is not alive – but still has the greatness of having lived... of having known the times in a life... and set foot upon the beautiful lake shores of the once Japan... and accepting them for what they were, whether filled with debris or beauty in an idea – he was one with all of it.

Now the dream is to be one like it was, but one must learn to accept the fact that the air has gotten both literally as well as metaphorically smoke clouded, the times have changed, there are new fires set daily, and to find some kind of Buddha is to find some kind of Buddha. No promises, but power preserved from the nothing sunlight/moonlight air to become a life past but its time's divine air of bliss in emptiness, and beauty in the fire burning and destroying and burning and making new chance, what one can do for their sense of peace, and the revival in a cause like the causes, the religions – should all be given account to but are mostly seemingly or defiantly NOT and people die in wars because of them – but the Buddha should just be seen as the writer of the Life Text. The view of survival and belief, but of the ultimate form and value, of LIFE, IN Being, and you can learn to form the value in the art of learning, modifying every idea for yourself, and not basing the facts of life on someone else's, yet learning them often, for bliss in the elegant space of emptiness does await and the gentle heir of the air seems to await, (I have learned this as some kind of sense), but you cannot quest for it. Make good while you are here, and with this philosophy you can realize even though peace in blank presence, that is a gratifying one – you are not there yet – so while you're here – imply upon yourself the task of making life a mission, maybe ease the pain of living... and the concept will be rewarded in your earth time reality... you were, and you are. You were a brunette and formed by flesh – now you are upon us as we sit and smoke and type – you are the air – you have found our memory of a life to be loved – and we know you inhabit our every emptiness.

This bit of writing more than likely, is the way only I look at the philosophy of Buddhism – much implied but I believe the notion reflects the aspect of my thoughts on Satanism, but more precisely and importantly – the notion I have formed to myself – and it took a fair amount of personal training and life events to form what I think if the majority of the people in America take and define for themselves in any text, Shakespeare and Nietzsche, Jesus or Mohammed – one must find an   INSPIRATION INSTEAD OF BELIEF – an inspiration to form the seeker's own beliefs, because as the world has seen throughout the human timeline – belief and commitment to a life serving a god can cause pain, and kill thousands as a basis for being too stupid to grasp that most religions were more than likely were originally intended to be upon their authorship – philosophy of the value in life, they call it a blessing – that word does not sit well with me – but in the most simplistic terms of relation – life is a blessing – but belief at too many times proves itself a hindrance. But it is a mystery to me why this want reprimands and kills the followers because the millions of injustices that go on in the world of human substance in reality – and not to take peace with them – but openly display to help the negative aspects about them vent – and the more they do – inspiration is built. Make these thoughts appear – it becomes an acceptance and an inner lull of the reality that no one can really do anything about anything – and I will rest one day. I do not believe I will see some kind of Buddhic circle – but on my death bed I shall not be frightened of the coming event – but will know I'll have been here, and saw the air move around me in the pitch black night air – a "blessing," I shall caress my paintings of Baphomet – and await the forever of inner becoming in a life lived and spent – the ultimate union of Bliss and Depth in Sweet Emptiness.

This is my trust in the personal modernization as I caress the face of my statue of Sakyamuni, and finger my mark of life and take pride in it, no matter the cost.

SATANISM:

Pretty red balloons entertain me. Red is with me. The hue of red was bladed with the destiny of black, a long time ago, blended into the dark so perfectly it became unseen – the power of red desire, passion, endeavor, -- and the black depth of pain is known to have the entirety of the blessed color of wont placed in it, very seeable to all in the beginning – but now only a few outstanding individuals notice the difference currently, and desire and proud red lie underneath black endless hue, of a truly deathless parting and parting to never latch upon again, a light behind, a light illuminating – it was an obvious contrast of shade in the beginning – now, only us – these Few Outstanding Individuals have the eye of the time that once was, and departed with the knowledge of notion to the way of loving life, but not getting by, not SURVIVING it, but taking the realistic sense of our humanity, loving it and using it, we can find ourselves because we have a good concept of the life we have, and our creations in this life. Loving our being as it is – human and base, human as base. A pride – nothing more. The dark with the rose, the black with red hose, the life in the blood, and the pride in what we are and die knowing what we were... here.

This blend of blood and depth, are what the masters of the Left have – not the slightest mark of a worthless life – BLOOD-DARK-LEFT-RESONANCE – the hue is so awe inspiring – its about twenty-nine years old – but confounds the Professor of the Left with its beauty – the tongue can not move – and he is the headmaster – we are around – but the man returns to look as more and more remains of his life to be took in his life – the notion on finding peace in eventuality – These Few Outstanding Individuals know the beauty in creation, and humanity no matter the cost – painters who mix red and black – the essence in life – and IT IS YOUR TURN to display as much as one wants, confounding the majority and offending fewer and fewer people – but making a mark of what they are – and sometimes it will be unnoticed to you for a living, but each one of these

Few Outstanding Individuals wears a visible mark in Red Black pride, and there are not many, but we notice them, and we greet our Fellow by not showing greeting, but by taking the pride in ourselves that there are others – however few. The Red BLACK mark will know it exists in the proud notion in your self – and another. The Left Hand Path can be more possible than one could ever think – but the Red Black Permanent establishment was never gone – the Red Black Permanent is a red sense of knowledge in where you are at the moment – and the knowledge that it will never come back, so make the most of it.

Die Verletzt Die Heilt. (That wounds). (That heals).

III.
JUSTICE IN KNOWING JUSTICE EXISTS

Sometimes – on nights like these – I feel the blood in circling through my veins, and I see it and I am glad it is there, I clench my fists until vein is visible as a flowing river, and I notice how much I enjoy my dream of life, but never of when in times I watch news and hear about some son of a bitch who threw an infant across the room because he was on crack, son of a bitch gave the kid life and permanent brain damage. How the mates gonna see you in the joint? They goin' to bust the fuck open your wasted head, time thief, bitch baby killer, heh heh…

And they are going to jam a sharp pushpin in your eyes until you cry, or maybe just bust open your motherfucking head. Sick little white nigger killed his kid.

I don't want to send you to death row, I don't like *us* killing one bit.

But here's my word to you – child wasting bitch ass freak, your defense lawyer knew you was gonna get sent to the pen in prison population, and he liked your hat so much you gave it to him, he talked and might have actually liked you. I ain't sayin I know this –

But I'd like to think his method was similar to mine, we are aware the dogs behind bars hard as a shit brick made even harder on any man who fucks with a child – and maybe we are both chuckling over pea-soup – thinking of you being tortured and brought to tears – maybe of your split child wasting identity of a nameless and pulverizing action on a baby who could not say your name, and now never will – you will not be given a mention in her history… heh heh… and I got your ass in my hands, tickling your brains which will be oozing slivers from your head against the rails… maybe he is thinking this – not precisely – but *EXACT* – *exactly the same sentiment* – justice for some pitiful bitch like you – American, red pus and blue substance of your brains running down the rails of black that hold so many that shouldn't be – baby killing weak eyes, rolled back in your head –

and a personal justice system in the knowledge you will never live again. And your punk ass needs to be on a plate of cannibal blood justice for a motherfucker. – The cannibal addiction to the site of blood gushing from a life that destroyed a 4 month old head, and we know you's gonna be blasted, your brains will ooze as inspiring as fireworks, you sick bitch crack addict who has absolutely no purpose but to die in pain, for what you did to your kid, she was never one of your sick life extinguishing selves, and now because of your weakness, she will never even get to make the choice of how to rebel against the pain you would have inflicted upon her throughout her life, no doubt – or she might have been the one that would slit your throat after you spent the night beating and raping her, but you threw her against the wall, and now she, the most deserving to give you this justice will never get to do this because she is not going to walk, or live as she could have, because of your vulgar deprecation in your self of a weak, weak piece of less than shit with an eight-ball preference over the life of someone who could have lived, you took that away from her, and now you gonna be in the pen, and both prosecutor and defense know you will begin the worst time of your pathetic excuse for a baby killing life – they gonna beat the shit out of your ass, then bust open your head with your right leg they tore off, and the police guardsmen will not interfere with this process.

Justice was done, and I will sit back and peacefully munch on a peppermint stick of gum,

Burn, bastard, burn.

But anyway, it is not a bad thing, still disgusts completely without ration, but I gain an inevitability of pride in humanity. I hate the man who hurt this child – and I like to think these thoughts of the defense and his thoughts over my pea-soup and lemon tea… and I don't mind my place in a suit and tie on days like these.– but core justice will blossom into a flower – black rose – that sheds the hour in the dominance of life who does not deserve to live – and I know I am not at the utmost understanding of this process, I'm just a lawyer from the ghetto, but I kind of give my nipple a little tug as a personal reward for realizing the longest but realistically shortest period of your waste and the more damning waste of your daughter's life – and in justice you will die of American lawfulness – but by the hands of the righteous drug dealing, pimp hustling, killing hands, who would NEVER EVER take their own life's worthlessness out on a kid.

You did what you did – and now you will suffer for it – and this is the type of day – I am proud to maintain and believe in the system of justice in the USA.

IV
Subject:

Let's get on the subject of why in these modern pop times of such human blessings as reality television and white boys saying they know what it is like and display it just as well as those with the naturalisms of a hard street ghetto began ghetto master in the most honest land black rapper, but why in these times of these such contradictions do we still say the way was made from a god of our choosing entity and base a lifetime around it? Most of the time involving a very attractive nun with no hose on her legs, who deprives herself from the idea of pleasure, much like reality television fans do not watch real TV shows, this Macbeth does not live in the common world briefly referred as "reality TV" world – she can't grow with the times – and she lives in a past so deceptive with the screwing up of a philosophy taken too literally, and perhaps every single day – she makes sure her dresses are no higher than knee-length, because she believes she is on a mission from the lord, and refrains from the love and pride notion which is sex. It is confusing that the earth does not evolve through the philosophy of the ideas and realities which are in it –

but the age of religion which has been around since practically the beginning of human thought – come with the few – and show your defiant existence that this is war until extermination on the practice of a life in belief in any thing besides philosophy stated as religion.

Defy Deny Declaim Devour... and praise not a thing more than your pride in your own humanity.

THE ART OF H.R. GIGER

Hit me...

Drain your face that's the place smack you hard like a throw down ace, jump at the image dream in the paint dream the mixed image of a multiple headed sage – come in, look at the work dream the significance of something only you and the artist knows... crack the code next time to find another – these paintings are a beauty with these realizations edged in and it resembles new passion ignited each time anew – like something you have seen that you never did before– but seemingly upon each sight it is something you did not previously know, and now you preciously do.

JOURNAL III

I.

I got this notion that's all bounded up in my head, right now – each part is transcribed as it entered my thoughts, I have them worked into my memory with no reason in the phrasing order transcribed, but the phrases are complete as I have burned them into my head:

1. Minor Example

Causal nature of an impediment of malcontent listen play time of you people, but it is so good, just listening to these mentally unique children, and keep demonstrating amounts of ambiguity because it says on the box you have to put on 14 quarts, then go and pay Asian Toenail Painting Removers Unlimited Natured conspiracy – and I am paid extravagantly, while this child makes fun of me, (we are trained to tune it out) and watch my cutesy tootsie toes wiggle. These are the people that ultimately most parents buy the phony wrist watch of he's in pain, I will need two thousand more dollars, to clock their children, 'well, I would but I do not have the time, and will immediately pay you, and buy drugs for my child.'

A therapy of talking in mixed language and hiding the fact that NONE of them, man or woman… heard most anything besides, 'I will tell you everything for a pack of smarties', but after the transaction takes place, they need to watch their toes wiggle or think about their outstanding abs, because child therapy is a tool for the masses – and every single college girl or grey haired fool is just one who prescribes drugs for your child that will make his hands shake or make him want to kill himself – mind you this was in my time – it may have changed, might not have, but this was what happened to me and many I met – worthless doctors who deserved the title less than nail salon attendants calling themselves artists.

And the only thing they honestly gave the boy or girl is a life-long-inevitable credit for a lifetime from busy parents whose laziness and their willing ability to tune them out, but make sure they pay a little attention, so they can hear the things they want to hear and prescribe pills for the beginning of a lifetime in the mental health system for kids… simple description of child therapy.

My parents were not lazy in the slightest, and I regret the demon I was to them. But the child psychiatric clinic was always very crowded, and had its own dealer, and kids should never be put on pills for some kind of implied mental illness, if a kid is troubled, you can take him somewhere he can talk, or talk to them (which my folks did), but the problems will only begin if mental meds are prescribed, unless a child hurts others physically. Kids are smarter than us, and these are my experiences with it – I don't subscribe to any mental health letter, but I read Freud… anyway – no 11 year old should be exposed to the junkie business of this kind of treatment. Their youth will be lost – I know this part.

2. Summation

64

Play the game ride along get here hard go there far.
Brought to mind, the human aspect of found relativism, not relativity, but relativism… the act of relation, the short description of the concept of child therapy relates to this because the riding along phrase would seemingly imply in this philosophy, to imply bending to their concept of normality, on you – but psychiatrists are the slightest in mind or perception because they take the form of those who believe they are normal people – and they hurt more than heal. This is not the ride I was referring to in ride along. This is not the only issue you have to never ride along with, minor in comparison to the things you need to do to ride along with, they are accounted by the second. It is imperative you must ride along the life of taking yourself and the world as you need to take it, and that one is the only person who can make the grade for their self, in themselves. Riding along is the way to redemption – take what life gives – make it because it is to be made… and it can be made good when one puts themselves on the ride of what happens – instead of trying to maintain a view or belief of another, in any sense.

II.
PITTSBURGH'S SENSE OF SOMETHING – THE WALDO
So little defining in the town, so little uprising because of it,
That's the way it is, that's the way it is.
WHERE WAS WALDO IN THE FIRST PLACE?
We made him in this town; people entity in the first place stenciled him so lightly these days it seems a challenge for him to be seen.

III.
Give the never admired position the flip of your own division…
Spines, man, *spines* – political refrain and gentle acceptance of me having a spine and being glad. King. King of sensible notion to do speak against all of your submission.
I am the King and you will forcibly massage my spine, but you are the purveyors of mainline normalcy in the dine on your dime, so you will be the ones who maintain my wealth.

IV.
Heavy research on the future time of the anomaly of a UFO invasion in the United States got me to thinking – hey I always knew the mix human and goat and AA battery fusion was going to pay our little system here a visit – I mean – we are here – and we have light as well as sustenance – why

did we never ever think invasion was obvious eventually – we should have had this common sense because us humans know well the likelihood in the invasion process.

I am the King, and they will come first to me, and know I am one from their place.

Kings will fall the world asunder.

This King will not be subdued because this King never submitted, and O, how the rest did.

V.

Please not be coming around these parts again, to put it country simple – we do not think you belong here. And you will be murdered if you shall return, that's what I am saying – no more tea-time for my little ways to try to get at the proper tea-time, because you try to take my way on the highway – instead of learning what oil you need for your automobile. Do you enjoy wasting my time – to put it country simple – emphatically/

You are more a murderer of me than the man who put a knife in my heart.

VI.

Sky line flavored eye drops

freshly caught taffy flavored crappy

I do not write about this much, because it brings unproductive depression
– but tonite –

Human kind's destruction of the environment is disturbing me.

We cake the lungs or fins of those who deserve to live far more than we.

It doesn't seem right...the oil spill in the gulf was contained this afternoon...

how many innocent gills or wings will be born before something else happens, because of a faulty business?

We say we will change and fix, but we will not, this is the negative aspect of the

natural defiance message in people, and you don't care. I care but realize my inability

to make an honest change about the sea life or any animal species.

So I would not be the least bit surprised if we kill more in a fortnight –

without realizing the value of any animal besides our species,

This time line of animal slaying is not recorded, because so little time passes

between each massacre – it would be impossible to apply a graph to –

just the promise that while we are here – the semblance of this crime will not end.

WITH THE REMEMBRANCE OF EACH BUG I EVER SAW

Busy busy – I have to be busy, I have to give myself the personal thought I am busy, have a life, etcetera. When I know my life is not a life. But I have recently learned to manage the things which come through my trip – or have – such as a murder of someone in my apartment – and the other little bugs in my head – did you know you can get tapeworms in your eyes from rat droppings? I do not have that and would not want to, I just have bugs in my head, and they do not bother me any longer – and I welcome them – the more the merrier so I have to accept every single day, as experience proves – one's mind is invaded by insects from the events one is bound to encounter – the event is the visual and the bugs are the access to the basis of surviving and living for the land. I have a deep respect for insects because they are not like any other order – and god knows there will never be an insect philosophy – but they do have one, bred into their blood, and are never questioned – but smacked away – maybe killed, but the idea is the insect will live to see every day – we kill some – but they are throughout and will extend significantly past our mortality, and all humanity that will be here. This is a respect I have for the life force which is the insect family. This is also, metaphorically minded, as in the insects are what happen to people. It is not in the mind to call everything which occurs in people's lives an entity not human, bad things are occasionally given a bug precedence, my deal is I give everything that happens insect relation, because each thing that happens, good, bad, indifferent – it will consume one, and will infest in one's day or night, life kills so why not just learn to take it instead of quashing parts on with a further destruction of the self, with always attempting to fix the larvae – Life is often as ugly as, or more – but in it you have to find the gentle acceptance, and freeze life larva within, instead of letting them (problems) squirm inside you – take them by living with them, and you might find the pride of survival in no distinguishing effect, the fact that you have a like mind and will survive for your time – but we still let the insects (events) we live, eat our minds. I am not saying I don't, but this is how I get around it. With the remembrance YET DISMISSAL of each bug I ever saw.

LIFE IN MY HEAD IN MY HEAD

Slow to the punch of a mediocre soda, not baaad… but only mediocre –
Give the pineapple princess the boast she deserves.

Have a medium sized flow of penetration, decide on the
depth of the cut, we sell band aids for every size cut of relation…

In my head. In my head.

Slimy drainage wasted years, bounty drive to the New York for the lights
—
Walk in circles around my "ghetto" in Pittsburgh at midnight.

Come here to me, dry up the seam – get the slime from the slope –
and become to. Strange dreams – sleep with the depth … and the hope.

In my Head. In my head.

The way of the day is the past of my dream, grate your dead –
the decision is the heart of the life bullet's throat based lead.

Hit me in the dry in the dead in my dream in my bed.
Remember the grates in the Alamo – crop the slight doe in Bambi's head…

In my head. In my head.

Time is just to date – time is just a human phrase – sometimes it works,
sometimes it doesn't. Now is the time for action… a time of personals lit with birthday
candles – rebirth, rebirth.

Very dry depth, very fathomed depth. Pry the genes, dismiss the schemes
—
Bend to the back. *Shake it shake it shake it.* Step to the left and
Face it*, step to the right and twist it twist it twist it.*

Lotsa dry in my mouth, losta air in my head – Sweet Jane they are the past and nothing else.
Quiet depth in every grain of air… self is the grant – it is what it is.
Future. Deliverance. Acceptance. It is what it is.

In my head. In my head.

Class dismissed.

A CONVERSATION WITH BARBARA
Slowly, Barbara, pull up to this car.
The man is very much enjoying the gum he is chewing/
there is a small puppy in the back seat/

there is something round, possibly a tossing ball there too.
The man driving this vehicle is about average height/
he is about five, six pounds lighter than me, Barbara.
He enjoys quiet nights in the country, and most
of his wardrobe is black with red stripes, Barbara.

His favorite things are to rationalize people driving/
he likes his odds of being right.

CHOICE

The mystery remains: is life the eternal mystery? The answer is very
detailed, and the species of the human race flavor it, with flavors of crosses,
Shivas, or any kind of this sort of detail... politics, views, legends, etc. The
latter is the most innocent in concept – being that the thing which labels
style or method. It is more common among the inference of simple choice
in humanity. A characteristic swayed by the world, and in no matter which
way one cloaks these concepts, the sentiment always remains – choice is
causal or good to have... but as a species, it can bring positive or negative
consequence, and one is not apt to take thought to the bad one – since
according to another simple aspect of humanity is bad things are negative
reactors much like good things are positive ones.
So, both "faith" as well as "choice" – are negative no matter the consequence
or reward, and both can be productive – faith in the sense of believing in
one's powers of what they can do, and doing it – accepting action as well
as reaction – choice more so because we have the choice to believe in
ourselves, and we do not consciously make the choice not to, but O we do
make this decision. And often we find our stated "strong" faith in something
other such as nothing but a tool of selfishness to help us get away and
escape – which relates in this way to the fact of drug or alcohol addiction,
as nothing but a weak tool to lead one into an easier, false acceptance of
what is as well as the falsity of being a lifetime user of a non-productive
substance, the forever trip away from reality – to the idea of some kind
of notion of a place we go after we cease to be besides the true beautiful
nothing which awaits, which is obviously an object of intense difference
among us, when in reality it should be no more than the simplicity we
accept and have learned so much from in this "modern day" world.
And if the words 'faith' and 'choice' were given precedence besides we
are the ones with the highest regard for both of them or we can vehemently
deny them – we are in fact choosing to apply either idea. But one does half
a personal accent that he or she calls denial – applied not in the sense of
feeling wrong about something – but it seems as the year's progress, denial
is seldom used as a description for these human feelings. The majority of

people in this world, or maybe in these states, experience denial to things such as a common faith in a higher eternity, or they use the denial trait that we used against it as an opponent... faith in life instead of the question of some higher power. Maybe SOME of us have shown progression in this sense, but too many of us still use it as a reason for living... and killing.

DEATH ROW FINALE
Poured in the salt, half a teaspoon of tomato juice and two grains of arsenic to kill you with.

Oven-time 46 minutes –

Now I would like to speak to you, about the good old life you lived, as I stated –
I am going to poison you to death – so please-
talk to me about your life.

Tony: I guess I would start at the very beginning but I do not want to do that,
just look deep in my eyes – I will become death –
spirit of perseverance...
brought about by your murder of me, I will become death before it becomes me.

STARE INTO INFINITY!

RELIGION:
Kill your dead. Kill them all again and again. Butter the bread with butter-jelly. Drink bloody wine. Find a chunk of lung. Bring it new breath. Take it out, nail it upon a wall, and breathe it dead. Kill it. Worship this murderer tribe, do it until your dead. And they will put a chunk of your lung into the moldy, red blood. Drink it. Choke on it. Die for it. Let my lungs get stuck in your throat, or my tongue licking your toes, they will infect. My tongue is a toe licker for your falsified ulcer/order. My lungs, like those dead before, will stop your life-incinerating self-righteous breath. This cannibalism – life's human condition? Only if that is what you make it.

VAN GOGH'S *"Starry Night"*
The portrait hangs on the wall, the portrait of the sky, the space, the eternity which is and will always be. Chaotically endeavored in spacious beauty, the movement, the movement. The painting hung on the wall, in the chaotic mess which was my residence for over a year. Many hours of contemplation into it's depth of art showed me something I never gave credence to –

70

the perfection that could become through a painting – and the philosophy it can create upon looking with a glance, so quick to become one with this work of a mind that saw the light of eternity in the movement a non moving forever and looked deeper than a polished, (though interesting in its own right), Mona Lisa. This is reality, and the reality so few can accept, this work of Vincent Van Gogh was the beginning of our human time here – movement, chaos, god, Satan, and all that would become, and all that will remain possibly upon each one of our deaths, no one knows this. But the movement in color, light and dark, illusion of the mind's faith in the glimmering starry night flavored with the hue of the darkness that will be, to this writer's mind – forever. This is one way of looking at it. But it speaks to each, and can be applied to each philosophy, but I feel this work portrays the depth, the dark, the human semblance of the human reality each one of us has the human will that none other has – to create – and though Van Gogh is long gone, this portrait of humanity as well as eternity speaks of the chaos and will in a life of each one of us... chaos in time, out of time, what is, was and always will be until we as a species cease, our ceasing to be, and in the most realistic sense – what will be after there is no more of us, and the world turns back to it's most natural state, which this artist displayed. Chaos in time, chaos is time, chaos in life, chaos in death – chaos in eternity... and the beauty in it, as well as the perfection in life so many see, and the ability for those who do not to find it. This is the impression of Van Gogh's "Starry Night" that I believe the intelligent as well as un-intelligent eye can benefit from. You do not have to be a scholar to find the depth of chaotic sensibility as well as reality to be accepted of what is, and what one can make, no matter what life perplexes one with.

JOURNAL IV
I.
LIFE IN MY HEAD IN MY HEAD II
Not requisitioned but aligned in your eyes.
Bribed in the depth and a user of the time
I can do this and I think you are somethin' that seems right.
You gabbed and grabbed a dove and I never saw a bird with your flight.

In my head. In my head.

Green pastures on fire forming blue flowers in their ash.
Something seems some things and I just have to ask:
The time in 97 when we conversed under Bodhi in Japan
What possessed me to draw the open box with my finger in the sand?

And, O, possessed you to place a lit red candle inside it?
Was this a kind of art – dripping wax all over my scribble – or analysis?
I have to see you a time again, I have to – buy you some bean – I insist.
Because I need your meaning, and I want to study you, you have to hear
my lifetime scream.
No intention of our bodies in the bed – but I do love you and want you –

In my head. In my head.

I don't seem 'NICE' to her or him.
But facts are just that – I'm a *real* human.

In my head. In my head.

II.
TO: DADA AND PATTY
C'mon Dark
1.
Burning in my mortal soul for you
Want you more than hell because only you I can't see through
Kings have dreams of bein princes and I have a dream of you
Now you know this – whatcha gonna do?

Telling whatcha gonna do, take a look at this good and Western Land
minded man.
This Dadaic heir beyond – that is my mission, to become and to brand
and I can guess, but know the Dada in the rain – and you as pure beauty
with
eventual refrain – somehow I know the voice of nothing is
everything – and I remember how I got here – and take pride in this Dada
echo dream as my own seer.

2.
Causal circumstance met with strength of desire instead of indifference
What does it make besides a space creation with your fingers?
Take strength in the sketch of time met and lost – sketch of spatial
countenance.
Time makes not a thing, age is impermanent death is the seam of lifetime
circle consequential dream…

It has never been put in a simpler phrase – the want in the life in the child
peace

Or in the ground in gravesite reign, space of been here, in the space between
and the living in the memory of an unbiased untimed speed
Someone needs to illustrate it so much better on the page. The notice of the
beauty in between has shown me human, and love sharpening life's blade.

Thought is just denial, space in time, love in life, bliss in depth of blank air
of dreamless sleep –

We are here and in it we must remain – and we can gain a countenance.
In this time of noticed space – and we can bust life's rhyme in our
mission...
To remain – to remain – how we got here matters not a thing but we are so
we can rise from our graves.
Can this mission be understood in your likewise living eyes of no refrain?

Dada but unlike any notion ever writ' in the power which is the life
And my wont and my where I have to look for space always find the time
C'mon Dark we can see the space so clear – in the dark space at midnight
–

Between the ceiling and where we sit, contemplating the division in
symphonic light delivery
And the moonlit sky, we can know the space and the fugue of our forever
time epiphany.

3.
Feelings are the thing I'll be addressing next in this tune:
Sly sightless sight of the never seen Dada as easy as a hex, but beautiful
as the moon
So something is there, the nothing in a lip touch jump in the nerves –
The nerves have a something – the trite something – but in bounty the
perfect air of the you or the forever front the leather I try to keep, but your
leather is more in touch than any mortal rhyme, like a Bach endeavor, the
knowledge in the space of an unseen line,
You will make it, and break to it never, or mask your face with hurtful
lace
You deal with life like me and O; your front is more than fine,
These were the feelings in the space between the notes of your front as in
your song of life...
But the well adjusted frame I hope mine will never receive,
But... whatever sense in self your parents were smart to give that you
received
Or the notice of what I can do about it, but I can get to me

Can I get to you, may I hope that you don't leave?
And further the Dadaic in my sense of this sense of heaven in the brail.
Between the brail for I know I'm not a blind man, but have a love for your
marks of life that will not fail…

Things been seen besides the dry well between
The water and the brick's vision of a moon every night seen
The reflection in the air, the reflection of the air, the sacred nothing but an
heir of perfect musk we will be feel. We can find us there.

4.
Try the drive into town, time to drink twelve or thirteen cups a coffee
Sit and stare fueled at the savage space of the tables in between
Sip and sip and sip touch the cornea of the savage Dada scene
And notice that nothing goes anywhere and reconciles with a time-peace.

Looking for it, this existential Dadaic air in the nothing
Saw your pupils graze in the delicate sighted breeze just we can see
Looked into the cold, cool in the depth of what it means
Depth/Defy/Devour state my mission to analyze everything.

And I analyze the space you inhibit and retain
And make an unlikely dream of Adam something from the union of Eve
and the snake
But when you make this sense, when you see what I'm saying
Trip the space in the fantasy of belief in what you look like in my dream
delaying.

Baker's choice engine noise and the nothing in everything
Things are becoming slowly as they should indeed be
This road to the Dada Lands is not one that's easy
But in the Dada Lands there is O, such a perfect breeze.

Will you, will you, will you see it with me?

MY LANDS
The Western Lands is a philosophy stated in prose by Egyptians, and
centuries later, an author. And is one that a person can vary on their own
terms, like just about every philosophy. Immortality is an important part
of it, but history as well. My view is we are all immortal because we have
been here, many of us such as William Shakespeare or Edgar Verese leave

a mark, so history implies immortality in this sense, but the key to the Dada door to my area of verification on the subject is – we all have been here – we all are truly our own in life and to other people, we need not be perfect playwrights or genius composers of symphonic air to leave with a ticket to the Western Lands, which in a way is a lot like a lottery ticket, so few win. So few die with so little pride in themselves or faith in a being who if one ever did exist, he died a long, long time ago. The thing that can produce a ticket to the Western Lands for these two aspects is key, you can in fact believe in some notion of a faith to get to the Western Dadaic Lands, but it is indeed of seminal importance that you appreciate the fact of what is here, what will make the air seemed flavored, the city lights or the corn field lit by the full moon as – what is, this aspect of grounding is the form of release fusion in life and death, and many on this road to death, find it in their spirit to become angry with the concept of belief to a point that is quite frankly unproductive and diminishing to themselves – this is not the way to Dada – and is the most broken glass shattered on the ground – the most self-destructive road to the Western Lands. Many Dadaists can look and learn from everything which surrounds them, and are in a perpetual state of learning... and we still live with common mortal pain that tries to crush us – but we know pain comes from nothing besides action – and every action before it is done – is in fact, an heir of nothing, things only happen to you if you do them – so mistakes, heartbreaks, murder, etc... are all begun in nothing, and once the something action fulfills the space of "before I or you did it" it was there, and now you did it. Road divides, and is indeed a challenge to take the correct one – but after thinking in the sense of Dada for so long, one can learn, however difficultly to ACCEPT it.

And to accept the destination of my Western Lands bliss in the air of not being more than a once was here

But the pride in this fact makes us unite our education of things happening, and digging so much so many of those who differ substantially with us. Fear, peace, life is, what we are, as well as the fact of our will, because we CAN. And we are on the road, and will retrace it in being here, and sometimes sight can baffle   but

produce   joyful/invisible/distraught/perfect/undivisive/value. As well as many tears, and the possibility of contentment.

ON THE FORMULA STATED IN PREVIOUS PIECE.

Let's graze the maze, let's bounce the sheets
Let's know the mirror mask of the most divine dream never seen
Let's go on a trip, to the muddy shores of the city

We can get this point of nothingness pride in pointless retreat.

Show me you, show me more, say the words in galore –
Because I know we can gain admittance and purchase in an everything
nothing store.

III.
TELL ME WHAT YOU GOT
What have you got, this night that will turn to the day, inevitably?
Or the perfection of the moonlight that is always in coming…
always to be returning?

Tell me what you got. Show me what you are thinking.
Give to me your time, the only time I ever seen, which
Did not *(never did)* prove itself to me as a time
used for knitting a flagrant veil for deception to yourself or a front towards
me and them
Tell me what you got. Give to me your thoughts as they give yourself to
your mind… let me learn your avenue of strength, and honesty.

> Tell me what you got.
> Tell me how you got.
> Tell me everything you saw.
> Tell me how it made you who you are.
> Tell me what you learned.
> Tell me what you keep.
> Tell me who you are.
> Tell me how you be.

*

You know, I know, what the world can do to those of us who can see it as
it is.
You know, I know, how it can hurt the eyes to look directly into the
sunlight.
You know, and me, the beauty of the winds that remain in the day *(in the
day)*.
We both know winds are in the night, and have the same descriptive
bounty,
or more, and more, because of their being under, us,
How are you, on this night with me, this night we touch the wind, the both
of us, in this dream?
Tell me, are we one, underneath the gleam of the moon, the starlight white
sheen?

> Tell me, how is this wind we touch this night.
>> Tell me, how you are.
> Tell me – can we be?
> Tell me – what you think…

As the wind and moon caresses your naked foot
do you feel a prominent hurt of the
perfect dream this night, this envy of time?
>>> that the night can't last Forever?
that this night won't last forever?
Tell me – are you taking the wind under this
moon as you never thought you
would ever look at something always
in coming as the shower of the nighttime perfection?
Tell me – are we here because it happened – or are we here on this night
–

because we are supposed to be?
>> Tell me what you are.
>> Tell me what you think.
>> Tell me how you be.
>> Tell me what you got.
>> Tell me – can we be?

*

*I know some things about you, and your physical self is an art of Life, and
it shows through you more than anyone this spirit has seen:*
(Brief but indeed worthy of analyzation):
Your hair is an auburn mist; it is such a perfect removed center to me,
making things that present
> themselves in the world which can hurt, or devalue life, seem
distant as the echo of a frog's croak
> to each of us on this city night, as we walk on the street…
> Your eyes are learned on the way of one
> who survives, one who makes a lifetime, a timeline of an
endeavored something that makes me
> want to breathe with you, the hazel marks of a life taught, a life
lived, a true sense of being in the
> world, and becoming as distantly right as a semblance of
remembrance to a dream of the perfect
> field, the perfect feel, the motioned continuance of a time that was
never encountered in the
>> time of a life anywhere, this time, this night, this feeling of the
>> earth made out of us, out of You and me… I never even gave the
>> slightest notion towards the motion of your eyes could bring me

as a reality,
and I know I am here, and I am gazing into this perfection, a way
of your own, not mine, but one I
have lived for, because of this night with you, this night you are
with me, your eyes shimmering the light, I am as unseen as the
pressure of the wind on our necks, I feel utmost this moment,
gazing and I was waiting... and as I am gazing, I am waiting to
go deeper deeper
into your eyes... and learning so much from them, organs we have
each in our physicality...
It is of immense value you let me learn of you, some things.

And I know these physical attributes are not your whole.
But I also know, they are perfect in their own space, just like
All you are, all you keep, all your rids all times lost, gained...
Each bit of your education proves itself on your face, and
holds part of your self-

S a m e
perfection   each
time you give me
a   glance   of   the
perfectly   lined,
perfect in time face,
And I feel proud to be where life put us this night, every time you
look at me.

Tell me where you are tonight.
Tell me how the wind seems right.
Tell me each thing you think.
Tell me how long this will last.
Tell me how you be.
Tell me – can I be with you?
Tell me something more.
Tell me, where to going we be.
Tell me – are you real?
Tell me – is this a hope, or a dream?

*

I know there is so much more than physical quivers that prove the perfection
of antiquated
And sentiment of depth within you,

Because every single second I spend with you on this true and
Perfection bathed depth I feel when on every single day
But especially this night I can gather an encyclopedic depth
And a knowledge beyond any book or human language reality…
Physical beauty to always keep the world waiting and guessing,
Trying to gather sense of commonality like none known, and the fact.
The fact is the jack because even though you revealed your true time
Retaliatory plan to me, I know I know know know, you are too grounded in
their common reality, and I know know KNOW to them I am seen as
Another one to you because your mission in the job is maintenance and
learning
For the $ and love it and hate it and hate you her him, and while I am there
with you
where we work, I maintain this aspect we know, because we know,
It's what we do, and that's that… but not a bit a glass of water to the
survival tactic
We know is the mission of the daylight time, a glass trying to drown us in
a false work ethic…

> But tell me, have we been on this night?
>> Tell me, what you see.
>> Tell me how you be.
>> Or more precisely, just keep sitting there,
>>> In the silence of who you are, say what you
>> should, or

Keep the silence, or break it, or continue your cycle of perfect being,.
And make the day, on this curb under street light,
And this yellow is what we are not,
And my time with you may in fact be short 123.
>> But tell me you will keep this remembered eve.
> Tell me – are you the one?
> Tell me – are you a dream?

Tell me – you rubbed strength on me with our kiss, please.

>> Tell me we are alive?
> Tell me – are we in this together?

>> Tell me – are you perfect?
> Tell me – is this night as true as it dominantly seems.

TELL ME WHAT YOU GOT.

IV.
REACTION TIME

I sit in a chair in a room in a place in a town in your face and I can't think of the last time someone looked at me that way. I give you more shoestring potatoes, because you requested more, and not a people has ever requested more potatoes from me. And you have asked in such a grand tone.

I remember the last time someone looked at me like this, but not even one moved me inside like you do, and I lived no longer than a dog years time of a life, and not a person made me cry for joy, who was in an heir of some kind of happiness, I do not live by normal physical reactions to emotions.

I am kind of at a good point in being, you made me cry when I was happy, and I will possibly laugh when you leave, this is good, this is good.

It proves I got me to my most confusing to the species I am a part of, but I don't feel like the opposite of my reaction – they are true…

Showing my personal pride in my goal, so I can fool all of you very easily, and I never would want to fool myself totally, but this reaction time shows my poignant learning that I am my own person, I take pride in being not one of their species who is a thing at all like any other of them. Yet immensely proud to be one, and you make me even prouder.

THAT'S IT

This is all there is, this is the end of the line, this is both the beginning and the end of a time. We are endeavored, we will continue to live as we will in this Dadaic reality which is an implied Buddhic Satanic Satiric concept of what it is to be alive, and live in the reaction to self which is more than they are, but knowing some of them know, and have a concept in its dream of natural beauty. There are those who do what they have to do, to get by... but too many of them do merely what they have to do, instead of doing what they can, defying their ability and stifling it. This concept troubled me for a long time, because I know many who could do more than their arrival in acceptance of where they are or where they were heading. There are both people like this in my great family, as well as ones by the has to be hundreds by now in the food mart I am a bag-boy in, which I have been confined to for the past 10 years, but I really have no choice, since I am too stupid for college. *Facts are facts.* The majority of them caused a sense of deep depression as in – where the hell is the future – and why are these people not making the most of their time as a human in their highest human being in life?

The idea of doing what you have to do to get by and the idea of doing what you can do, well, to me – they do not intertwine in the time in a life to me. Say your goal in life is to help people, and to be around them and learn their value – this is not bad – if it is what you can gain your highest sense of a good life from. BUT – I have seen and see every day good minds, minds who are barely 19, for example, who have an understanding of such things as the writings of Nietzsche, and a knowledgeable one , who could do so much more than they have confined themselves to – but I realize I can never do one thing about it – but the young minds with this intelligence in their minds are just as bad as the 67 year old people there who have been there (in the mart) since 19, and are only now realizing their own worthless stance in life – this does not affect me in the least way anymore with feelings of lost being. I know now even if I do try to change something about another – it is a goal that is unachievable... and I also do not know anything about the other, even friends or family – so their goals may make sense if I were them, I just have a really hard time viewing the concept of not making the most one can of themselves and taking the latter road of dismissal of productiveness and self-appeasing belief with much positive acceptance when there could be possibility to make so much more out of themselves, this concept is not one I never find myself in – in fact – I know it well. But I just don't understand, and there are people who have college doctorates who can't find work besides a food mart... and this future is not one that has no possibility of being mine, but the more I get in my head, and the more I gain to try to challenge me with, and leave my current state which causes a lot of pain in me, and will continue to for some time no matter the goals I do achieve, because to learn is more than distraction and the more valuable things one has in their heads takes a lot away from the current reality they are condemned to, to the point of benign acceptance of even taking a fake first class ticket on the ride one is on while on this trip called this life, and I know there are many in it who have done this, and I just will not. Experience makes a person; the dull sword of people like this in them is really not my matter or business for my blade, which is by no means too sharp to begin the duel with anyway. There is nothing I can do about it. No one understands anything about any other person's life or ideas. This has been proven in my life as well as in others in the America and the world countless times, and will continue to, I am sure. But I will never refrain from my goals, and I will make it, no matter what another tries to prove or even proves about me, I know they will not understand me in the slightest, and I am not one of them. I am me.

System is not connection.
Correction is never permanent.
Connection can be, but pointless reaction isn't a ways to its dependence
Try! Try! Do not subside to reflection...
for it causes too much memory dissection...
and will fool you into a crass lifeless false force who has seemingly learned
too much from a beginning biding of the hour – but in the end is no more than a dissident acceptance!
TRY! TRY!

*

But, in all reality I know – I will cease to work in this little food mart eventually, and it will not cause an end to pain... though it will increase sufficiently my value in myself to quit... but I know, I know – that it isn't all there is, and challenge will continue to present itself day to day. I have a lot of, I guess it would be called ambition, or maybe sadomasochism, because I always feel the need to strain myself for more... the reason I never did anything except the simplest jobs in the mart, and will still is because I really do not need memorizations of codes and ways to operate the calculator register to take up the space in my head that may dispel some value I can learn of life, and the ways I need to show my anger towards things that happen in the world, to try my damndest to make a way for me where I can learn to actually work as well as distancing me from them, so I do not have to even speak to them unless the situation is with one I like and I feel I need to comment on her red hair and green undershirt, or the best rock n' roll songs... though it does seems as the years go on and I have not elevated from my meat packingness, these people seem to be becoming less and less real to me. I do not like the most of them there much, but I do not hate them either – just dirty, bent, deviant pennies in the wishing well of the lost is my view of them.

But I know that's not it, there will be more/such is life. It's going to be something else... I really am not planning on finding things to complain about when I get out of the nowhere league retail situation because I will always have the bludgeoning memory of too long in it, though I have made friends there.

*

The times they are a' changin,' and nothing is permanent – I use these thoughts to console me and I will survive, though this life I have lived in all aspects in itself has tried to kill me faster than my afternoon joint and shot of whiskey ever will. But that's it, that's all, that's all there is, life challenged the hell out of me and I know it will continue to, and I know, in reality even, NOTHING, not even love, stays exactly the same. Things move on to better themselves, in each way they do this, even in ways that can be negative in concept to the single life of a person. William Carlos Williams said in one of his fine poems – *"no ideas but in things"* and that was his honest view and belief. I amend this statement to my view of the life situation by my statement – *no act in the fact of life without progression.* This concept applies to us humans, and in these times, we apply this fact to us and it moves us forward. The concept is the one which nature has implied since the beginning in the animal kingdom, and the attack and consumption of a moose, say by a cougar... and we humans have to learn to apply this concept to us as individuals and what our life contains. The moose died because of the beauty in nature's art which is the hunt, and kill... and only the strongest survive through use of the beings that are not necessarily negative, the cougar had no grudge against the moose... but saw him as a way to provide his continued life, and the cougar attacked and maimed and killed him. The way one of us must apply this to our lives is not in the literal sense whatsoever... we are humans, and we have the pride in what life is that the cougar does not for his... therefore we are lucky enough to have pride in others lives as well as our own, and we must never take a life, EVER. Even us who are the most respectable of this aspect do, myself included, being that we for the most part are not vegetarian, I wish I could be at times, but I just can't, and if I was it would not stop the want of meat by the common public... it is NOT the hunt's beauty we take from our food, and hunters are the most despicable because a side of deer prepared even is less of an expense than hunting gear, they take pleasure in killing in the human way, the animals who did them no harm, so they can tell pretty Janey or handsome Joey how they did it, and the meat is so good and plentiful, the concept that these deer, or whatever deserved to live more than those who killed them, does not even come across their minds, it is not, it is not in the least the hunt of nature these people imply upon their self-service so unappreciative. Murder is never justified.

But the cougar idea is one we must imply emotionally on all levels, and on levels beyond emotion that really do not have individual names there are so many of them, but each little inner feeling is a million-fold notion under one word – survival. A lot of time it can seem a long time in coming, but assholes always end up paying their dues even if it is in the end of their lives with the knowledge of a pointless trip through mortality and the fact that the majority of people did not like them while they were here. Sometimes it can work, and we can watch or have the knowledge that our enemies are suffering with themselves, burning in their own pit of poignant rebuttal of the misfortune or annoyance like they did to us, they will burn. They'll get theirs, I have seen this happen in my life with just about every single one who tried to break me but were unsuccessful – the nature mentality reigns, only the strong survive, and the strong will in one way or another win and get to put on an air of joviality while watching those who tried to be an end to a certain aspect of ourselves we hold with pride, but they are burning, and they were not a deflection to our state of life in any way... this is how we have to imply the hunt of nature and the slaying of those who are lesser than us... and we must also use them as a necessary point of ingestion for ourselves and take from them what we can, life put them there... yes they have life... so they have to deal with it, and they can't, therefore we chew slowly the fresh moose meat of the fact that we can and they are lesser, and even if they are not suffering at the moment, we must know in our minds and in our hearts that they will suffer eventually, possibly not by our hands, but they will suffer... they will burn, and maybe eventually one day, we'll see them on the street begging for a nickel, and we can laugh in their face with implied vampiric teeth, and look deep into their living dead eyes and say – *"who won?"* No recompense for those who tried to be some kind of deterrent to our pride as us. We will watch them burn and laugh, know we won, and know we are so much better than even their kindest dream of themselves.

Bring it on, bring it hard, and shove it in my eyes

Dream of what you never were; fill your time with lies,
Say you want to talk, then something in you will realize,
The talk I give to you is an annihilation of yourself, and inside the more
you die.

What's the word jim? Is the word belief caused conceit? Back inside the
gym...
Makin the game of weights you throw to the floor, but provin life's weight
is somethin you can't lift,
Your mind is slow, your health is low: all we have in common is this,
But my time in my life is curled like a lift less reverence,

So bring it hard, I am a bounce remaining in refrain,
The sonata in my symphony is more divine than your waste
And I'm here until I split, for stil a little bit, I try to never waste it though
break it at the base
You're a pigeon turd in the Allegheny river, and you will fake it instead of
make it,
And to fall straight down, wasting your face with see through grace.
And I can get where I'm headed... and know you ain't headed nowhere,
And no matter what you think, you are nothing to me, so I don't care.
I may see you around, and I never may again, but either way it won't cause
your desired effect for my end...
Because my weapon is my ability to handle my life, in my head, in my head,
and have an open rebuttal of your made mess and my direction of these
towers to OPEN FIRE! and to raise my own time against the alive ones
who are dead.
To show their dead selves to the ones who defile their grave
To cancel their notions and make their time nil til' their alive but dead An
ended waste!
*

I am aware these statements are probably vain with no sense of credence
to much more than besides a goal I wish I could leave behind, maybe to
be remembered for, but they are in fact a goal I believe I make, so all I can
honestly state with them is my unbending will to try, and try to get the most
I can out of my life, the ones on them are my honest view, so what else can
I do, but **TRY! TRY!**

*

Then, there is you. Then there is you, that I want more than I know I have
ever wanted any single person in my bed, to know me, in my head, in my
head.

And this possible equation still presents itself to me rather frequently, but the things which happen to me, and seem to keep happening in my life… a lot good, and a lot bad, have forced me to come to a more actionable towards the goal fulfillment I set for myself since the time I was almost killed in the year 1997.

I spent a long time looking at you, and your beauty always enticed me to try to "hit" on you, like they call it. I spent a long time punching the brick walls of outside buildings every time my "hit" was countered with the shotgun blast of rejection from you. I spent too long occasionally audibly, sometimes murmuring to myself with just as much or more painful shrapnel removal of the things I was saying so I could have some kind of personal release of being blasted with your refusals… over and over, and time and time again. I died more every single time it happened.

And I am not even suggesting I have found a "one" to love me in the loving sense, and I am not saying I no longer ache from this kind of loneliness.

But something extremely important and valuable happened to me which I learned from the overall lesson I learned by your countless denials. I learned I am not one who is equipped in the least for interaction with women when I have the goal of someone to love, someone I would love to learn to love from, immediately in my head, in my head. If a woman who has something I am intrigued by in this sense comes to my life, and believe me, they do, they do… I do not initiate any conversation, I do not try to learn what their goals are, if they are beautiful (as just about all of them are), even if they have a strength learned from this life trip I respect… I do nothing to even show them the slightest bit of something such as respect. I do not disrespect them; I just do not do anything initiative for my hopes of the two of us. I have learned even if I do not wave my freak flag, (or more aptly, my love for my life, and most life in general or express my discontent in what life has tried to break me with, as a learning experience) even if I do not let the slightest indicator of my content or discontent show – there is something about me that the woman finds repelling if I try to "get" to "know" her. I do not even try anymore. Yes, when I see someone I would want to be with, it still hurts, it still sometimes remains for a few days, not because I am confronted with their refusal, though. And this pain does not take anything out of me anymore. As a matter of fact, it very, very, rarely even registers any longer. I see you, I saw you, and this happened, and I accept it. I saw you about an hour ago, and this happened, such as it does… but the point in the feeling is that I had enough in me not to even try to "hit" on you, but I saw you and felt this way, so the only implication by me was dismissal, and in this hour's time, I really am not bothered even in the slightest by it, and I will use it for fodder to continue to remain at this point of taking pride in the possibilities life offers, because I am pretty sure I will never have one of the beautiful women that shadow my life. The shotgun of refusal did not even get to be loaded, I did not even dodge the bullet, I was just out of it's range before it was even removed from the case, and you never knew the intention, so in this sense, I saved more of me from dying from the blast. If you come along, I am not suggesting I would not try again… but the introduction of the relationship idea will NOT be put into action by me. If you come along, you come along… I know I have what it takes to survive either way. The only relationship I ever had caused me to trust the notion even less, and gave me a horrible memory. I'm not giving up, I am just taking it if it shows itself to me again, but if it does not, there is so much more one can make of their lives.

In a way, in my way, I have learned to deal with my pain through distraction and dispelling of their ways which are at the root, despicable and hurtful and give challenge to so many of us who are not them. In my way, in my way, this is my Dadaic Satanic stance on that issue. Do as much as I can, try to help when others are in need of it, but with the issue that my survival to my natural death is the goal I have to keep in me.

Life comes around one time, and is the highest reward of time, it is my initiative to make the most I can out of my time here for me, and know life is mine, and my life is beautiful.

This Was Semi Important:

This is my time, these statements were me.

This is my life.

These are my goals.

This was my pain.

This was my Peace.

To me: These statements are very important.

That's it.

FIN'

(Thursday, August 19, 2010)

Quote of William Carlos Williams: "no ideas but in things" used in

final essay "That's It" from his poem "A Sort of Song"

Used from "The Collected Poems Of WCW: Volume II"

(pg. 55)